T0293137

Radek Kovács
František Ochrana

Nudging towards Health

CHARLES UNIVERSITY
KAROLINUM PRESS 2023

KAROLINUM PRESS
Karolinum Press is a publishing department of Charles University
Ovocný trh 560/5, 116 36 Prague 1, Czech Republic
www.karolinum.cz
© Radek Kovács and František Ochrana, 2023
Set in DTP Karolinum Press
Printed in the Czech Republic by Karolinum Press
Layout by Jan Šerých
First English edition

A catalogue record for this book is available
from the National Library of the Czech Republic.

This monograph was created and published as a part of the support
system for faculty monographs of the Faculty of Social Sciences,
Charles University in Prague, as an output from the Specific Higher
Education Research (SVV) project (supported by the grant SVV 260 596)
and the Grant Agency of Charles University (project no. 70222).

ISBN 978-80-246-5503-1
ISBN 978-80-246-5512-3 (pdf)

The original manuscript was reviewed by Jan Mertl
(University of Finance and Administration, Prague)
and Stanislav Klazar (University of Economics and Management, Prague)

Contents

Introduction

The subject of this book is the "nudge." If we want to discuss the procedure of a nudge, then we are talking about nudging. The concept of the nudge is relatively new (see Thaler and Sunstein, 2008), although it finds application in various areas of social life. The key to the concept is the idea that the appropriate nudge can influence a person's behavior by encouraging them to re-evaluate their priorities in a way that they voluntarily change their behavior, thereby bringing them personal and social benefits. One of the most important areas of modern society where nudging finds use is healthcare.

This publication examines nudging in relation to selected health policy issues such as preventing obesity, malnutrition, and type 2 diabetes. These diseases are obvious, complex social problems that affect the health of the entire population, public expenditures on health care (see e.g., Maaytová, 2012; Maaytová, Gajdošová, and Láchová, 2018; Medveď, Nemec, and Vitek, 2005; Mertl, 2015), and the cost-effectiveness of such expenditures (Vrabková and Vaňková, 2015; Mertl, 2016). They can also affect the government's tax structure (Klazar, 2010; Mertl, 2012; Mertl, 2013).

These health issues have multiple impacts. Take the case of obesity, which poses a serious challenge to public health policy. Reducing obesity levels in population can certainly be affected by nudges. Obesity can lead to a number of serious and potentially life-threatening conditions, such as type 2 diabetes, high blood pressure, coronary heart disease, various cancers, and strokes. Obesity can also affect a person's quality of life and lead to social and psychological problems such as social exclusion, isolation, depression, and low self-esteem.[1] A rational person is able to acknowledge the benefits of adhering to the principles of a healthy lifestyle and the consequences of violating them. However, the puzzling question arises as to why the incidence of civilization diseases in the Czech Republic, including type 2 diabetes mellitus, is growing. Why do we see a discrepancy between the ontological side of the problem (real human behavior) and the behavior of the theoretical *Homo economicus* axiom, when we expect people to act purely rationally based on *Homo economicus* rationality.

From the perspective of the *Homo economicus* axiom, which dominates mainstream economics, it seems self-contradictory that people generally know that obesity is detrimental to them, and yet in reality they do not behave as the economic behavior theory based on the *Homo economicus* axiom predicts. Speaking philosophically and methodologically, the relationship between substance and phenomenon lies behind this discrepancy. As it turns out the economic model of individual's rational based on the *Homo economicus* axiom fails to properly explain the discrepancy between reality and expected outcomes. With this in mind, we have set the following objectives:

Examine the ontological and epistemological foundations of human behavior based on the notion of *Homo economicus*.

---

1   As numerous publications show (See e.g., Rybka, 2007; Svačina, 2010), obesity is one of the factors leading to the development of type 2 diabetes. Almost a tenth of the Czech population (more than 900,000 inhabitants) suffers from diabetes mellitus. The vast majority of cases are type 2, an incurable, lifelong, metabolic disease. In patients with type 1 diabetes, insulin is absent. Not only diabetes harms the individual, but also the society as a whole. According to expert studies, the disease shortens life expectancy by 30 to 50% depending on the type (Rybka, 2007). The risk of developing type 2 diabetes is more than 50% for children of a type 2 diabetic and nearly 100% if both parents have type 2 diabetes. At the same time, it is alarming that every year about 60,000 people in the Czech Republic are diagnosed with diabetes, and about 22,000 patients a year die of this disease. (See EUROZPRÁVY, 2020: Kolik bude za deset let v ČR diabetiků? Asociace prozradila víc. [How many diabetics will there be in the Czech Republic in ten years? The association revealed more.] Source: https://eurozpravy.cz/domaci /zivot/kolik-bude-za-deset-let-v-cr-diabetiku-asociace-prozradila-vic.fe05294c/ (downloaded on March 2, 2021). The rate of adult obesity in the Czech Republic is one of the highest in the EU and has increased by more than 30% over the last 15 years. About 20% of Czech adults are obese; well above the EU average of 15%. (See https://ec.europa.eu/health/sites/health/files /state/docs/2019_chp_cs_czech.pdf). Only about 61% of Czech adults engage in at least light physical activity each week, less than the EU average (72%). The rate of overweight and obesity in children is increasing. About 17.5% of 15-year-olds are overweight or obese (see https:// ec.europa.eu/health/sites/health/files/state/docs/2019_chp_cs_czech.pdf). The government could improve this situation with an appropriate "nudging" policy.

Explore the theoretical and methodological basis of the nudge and define nudging in terms of contemporary scientific discourse.

Define the nudging tools in the paradigm of prospect theory using content analysis of the literature and examine their use in health policy setting, with an emphasis on diabetology. In doing so, conduct a systematic review of the literature on nudging as it relates to healthy eating.

With these objectives in mind, we pose three research questions:

Research Question 1: What are the epistemological foundations of the concept of human behavior based on the notion of the *Homo economicus* axiom and what are the theoretical and empirical foundations of nudging?

Research Question 2: What are the differences in the paradigm explaining human behavior of classical economic theory and prospect theory?

Research question 3: What health policy tools can be used for food nudging and how is nudging reflected in contemporary scientific discourse? What do the research conclusions mean for public health policy?

Apart from general scientific methods we used content analysis of the scientific discourse focused on the nudge found in the literature and a specification method for defining the elements of nudging in healthcare (specifically, in diabetology). The result is a systematic review of the literature, contained in the third and fourth chapters of this book.

The main contribution of this book is that it provides an analytical-systematic view of the current state of scientific discourse on the nudge published in scientific journals indexed in the Web of Science and Scopus databases. It clarifies and compares the theoretical and methodological basis of two basic concepts that are used to explain human behavior, namely the concept of *Homo economicus* and the prospect theory of the nudge. From a comparison of the two theories, we formulated conclusions that provide stimuli for further scientific research. The book also has practical benefits: it will provide help in the public policy formulation process (especially health policy) because it analyzes the effectiveness of various tools (nudges) in the field of health care. Based on analysis of individual nudges, it makes general observations and provides recommendations for public policy.

1. Human Behavior in the Traditional Paradigm

1.1 Defining "Human Behavior"

Human behavior is a social phenomenon. We understand human beings as actors responding to stimuli in their social and other environments. In general, their actions can be both intentional (i.e., targeted) and can be unintended (unplanned). We see that these are two different methodological approaches. In our publication, we will present the concept of human behavior based on behavioral economics, and we will consider the impact of Kahneman's concepts of "fast" and "slow" thinking (Kahneman, 2011) on Thaler's and Sunstein's concept of the nudge (Thaler and Sunstein, 2008). We are of the opinion that human actions can be both intentional and unintentional (instinctively conditioned). However, human behavior, as a whole, is a mix of actions (intended and unintended) that manifesting themselves as a reaction to external stimuli and serve as feedback to the stimulus source.

From an ontological point of view, human behavior is a complex phenomenon. The complexity is reflected in the diversity of the approaches of individual scientific disciplines to its study. Scientific disciplines—such as cybernetics, psychology, and economics—offer various perspectives. From the cybernetics point of view, human behavior is feedback on certain stimuli in the environment (Wiener, Ashby). From a psychological-behavioralist point of view, human behavior is operantly conditioned (Skinner), that is, actions and reactions are conditioned by exposure to environmental stimuli. However, neither psychology nor economics completely agree on the basis of human behavior. Freud's deep psychology offers yet another completely different psychological view of human behavior. For an overview of these different psychological views, see, for example, Hunt (2007).

The economic theory of human behavior is crucial for our research because the concept of nudging originates in economic science influenced by experimental psychology. Ludwig von Mises's voluminous book, *Human Action* (Mises, 1998), which deals specifically with human behavior, is of a great importance to the economic conception of human behavior. Mises created the praxeological theory of human behavior. He relied on the tradition of classical rationalism based on the work of René Descartes. Classical rationalism is characteristic of mainstream economic theory, where the key axiom is that human beings are in reality a species of *Homo economicus*: rational beings who pursue their own interests (Mises, 1998). Mises believed that economics deals with purely rational actors and that human behavior is necessarily rational.

Mises insists that human action involves making a choice and that the choice is a rational one at heart. According to Mises, human behavior "comes from the same source as human thought," and can be described using praxeology. To him, the theories of praxeological reasoning are not only perfect and irrefutable but are in fact mathematical. They predict the reality of action as it appears in life and history with the full rigor of their apodictic (self-evident) certainty and irrefutability. Praxeology offers accurate and precise knowledge of real things. The starting point of praxeology is not the choice of axioms and the decision about methods of procedure, but rather reflection about the essence of action.

Mises criticized the naturalistic view of human behavior. His view is a critique of the naturalistic behavioral traditions of Wundt and Skinner, as recorded in the history of psychology (see, for example, Hunt, 2007). Mises is critical of naturalism and of authors who are eager to construct an epistemological system of the sciences of human action according to the pattern of the natural sciences. He vehemently rejects this approach, known as "social physics" (Neurath).

Mises considers the science of human behavior to be aprioristic (based on self-evident principles) and not empirical. His beliefs are based on Kant's aprioristic concepts, judgments that cannot be verified in any way. The subject of praxeology is therefore the study of human behavior as such. Praxeology provides us with formal knowledge of human behavior. The statements and conclusions of praxeology cannot be verified or refuted. Mises concludes that no experiments can be performed in the field of human behavior. His conclusion that praxeology is impossible to verify has been criticized by positivists. Karl Popper disputed that its tenets are impossible to refute.

However, we think that both mainstream economics and Mises's conception of human behavior have similar ontological and epistemological starting points: Cartesian rationalism and Cartesian epistemology.

1.2 Human Behavior from the Perspective of the *Homo economicus* Axiom, Cartesian rationalism, and Epistemology

When mainstream economics was taking shape, its leading figures decided to model economics after physics—in particular, Newtonian physics. Newtonian physics explains the mechanical behavior of macroscopic bodies moving at speeds close to zero, speeds that are negligible compared to the speed of light. Metaphorically speaking, the ontological object in Newtonian physics is the world that we encounter as people on day-to-day basis.

From an epistemological point of view, Newtonian physics is based on classical rationalism, i.e., the Cartesian type of rationalism, established by René Descartes in *Rules for the Direction of the Mind*. Cartesian rationalism is based on the idea that firm conclusions can be drawn using logic, working from explicitly defined premises. Using Descartes' method we can build an axiom-based deductive theory. An axiom is an a priori valid thesis and does not need to be proved. Axioms must be internally indisputable and independent. That means that in a given system there cannot be axioms contradicting each other and that it cannot be possible to derive an axiom from another axiom or axioms. From the point of view of scientific laws, axioms can be considered laws that are not otherwise derived in the logical system. However, it is possible to derive theorems from axioms. Theorems are laws that are derived within a system. A theory created this way is an axiomatic theory, a formal theory requiring a formal proof in order to demonstrate its validity. This method and its procedures are characteristic of mathematical theories (see Hilbert's calculus).

The principles of axiomatic-deductive theory are applicable in many scientific disciplines. One of the axioms of classical economics is the idea that humans are *Homo economicus*, meaning that a human actor is a perfectly rational individual possessing perfect knowledge, making rational decisions with the intent to maximize personal gains, and minimizing losses (costs). In mainstream economics, the axiom of *Homo economicus* is the starting point for explaining human behavior. In the logic of Cartesian rationalism, human action is purely rational activity. Assuming human beings are *Homo economicus*, it is possible to explain an actor's action rationally. In reality, however, the assumption of rationality leads to trouble. If we were to agree with the Cartesian way of thinking, rational action requires perfect knowledge of all relevant facts. That would be only possible with knowing all the given circumstances of initial premises apply, for so long as those conditions remain unchanged. That is impossible in reality for two reasons: ontological and epistemological.

From an ontological point of view, the vast majority of systems, including human society (and therefore the economy), are dynamic systems. Dynamic systems are characterized by the following ontological features: instability, imbalance, irreversibility, and nonlinearity of developmental trajectories. Dynamic systems change over time and tend to be unstable. Examples of dynamic systems are economic cycles and the unpredictable (or difficult to predict) behavior of financial markets, as well as the spread of pandemic diseases.

From an epistemological point of view, the behavior of complex systems cannot be explained using Cartesian epistemology. Only those who believe in the omnipotence of the Enlightenment would think that dynamic systems can be as reliably managed as deterministic systems and that epistemology is fundamentally wrong. To understand the behavior of dynamic systems, it is necessary to turn away from Cartesian epistemology and move on to non-Cartesian epistemology. The Newtonian paradigm, based on mechanical determinism, breaks down the boundaries of mechanics. It cannot be used to study dynamic social systems without the risk of oversimplification. Newton's paradigm presupposes that the world (and society as a subsystem of it) is by nature a system that naturally oscillates around a state of equilibrium. This idea echoes in mainstream economics with Adam Smith's "invisible hand." Walras's idea of general equilibrium was also inspired by Newtonian mechanics and the idea of "systemic equilibrium."

One characteristic of non-dynamic systems is that we can rationally predict their state at any time. This is because coincidences do not significantly interfere with the causal chain in such a system. Changes in a non-dynamic system can be reliably predicted because predictions are based on deterministic (strictly given) causality. The explanatory paradigm of non-dynamic systems considers nonlinearity and instability to be randomly distributed phenomena. They are the result of noise and transients. Malfunctions in the functioning of a non-dynamic system are considered natural, occurring in the long-term, otherwise essentially balanced evolutionary development. For example, the economic theory of business cycles relies on the idea that periodic changes in variables lead to a change in the cycles of the economic system. A chaos is a random phenomenon, because it is a failure without a cause in the particular system. The malfunctions are therefore the result of dysfunction at the epistemological level, such as improper regulation.

The primary causes of instability in dynamic systems are not found at the epistemological level, but in the very nature of these systems. If we do not realize this, we will fall victim to the illusion that this instability can be prevented by simply correcting or improving regulations, enhancing information flows, and eliminating the effects of chance occurrences. However, coincidence and its effect on the stability of dynamic systems cannot be eradicated. We can only acknowledge that even a slight co-incidence (e.g., the butterfly effect, Lorenz) can destabilize the system and lead to its bifurcation (i.e., splitting and disintegrating). With re-spect to dynamic systems, a mechanical-deterministic worldview must be replaced by a different theory, the evolutionism, which can explain the influence of a chance on developments.

We do not mean to reject the idea of *Homo economicus* in the economic and social sciences in its entirety. We should only keep in mind that the models and theories based on this axiom have limitations and are built on particular assumptions. One of the key assumptions, in addition to the a priori rationality of behavior, is that economic actors have perfect information (Meričková Mikušová, Jakuš Muthová, 2019). The difficulty with this assumption was noticed by Herbert Simon, who formulated the concept of bounded rationality. He noticed that the theory of humans as *Homo economicus* is unrealistic. Cartesian rationalism cannot fully explain human behavior and its consequences. Essentially, the Cartesian type of rationality can be used successfully in cases where the premises and con-ditions remain unchanged (Ochrana, 1998); sufficient in the context of Newtonian physics and Euclidean geometry, but it no longer in the con-text of Einsteinian physics and Riemannian geometry. Likewise, it can be said that the Cartesian type of rationality can support economic theories based on *Homo economicus*, but it cannot account for "non-rational" factors affecting human actions. The response to this insufficiency was the emergence of behavioral economics and the concept of the nudge.

2. Nudges and Nudging

2.1 Behavioral Economics and Prospect Theory: The Theoretical and Methodological Bases of the Concept of the Nudge

Paradigms are crucial in science (Kuhn, 1970). According to Kuhn, a paradigm is a generally accepted result of scientific research, which in a given community of experts at a given time represents both a model of a problem and a model for its solution. A paradigm is thus a way of solving a given scientific problem. According to Kuhn, a scientific revolution entails a paradigm shift. The initiation of a scientific revolution occurs when an anomaly emerges (Kuhn, 1970), that is, when a new phenomenon cannot be explained using the current paradigm. Such an anomaly was recorded by Preston and Baratta (1948) during their experiments with the behavior of people at auctions under conditions of uncertainty. They concluded from their experiments that people overestimate low probabilities and underestimate high probabilities. This led them to doubt whether the existence of *Homo economicus* was axiomatic. A new explanatory paradigm began to emerge, currently known as behavioral economics. If neoclassical economics based its theories on the assumption of "pure" rationality, behavioral economics takes into account other psychological factors that influence human behavior. Human behavior began to be perceived as a series of complex choices (Baláž, 2014) that are accompanied by risk and uncertainty (Baláž, 2009). With his concept of bounded rationality, Simon (1947) pointed out the need for a new non-economic approach to the choices an actor makes.

The pioneering papers that brought this new paradigm to economic science were the publications by Daniel Kahneman and Amos Tversky

(Kahneman and Tversky, 1979, 1984; Tversky and Kahneman, 1974, 1992) and their collaborators (Fox, Kochler, Riepe, Slovic, and others). Their experiments with decision-making under conditions of uncertainty and with choices between the present and the future have shown that the behavior of *Homo economicus* is not purely rational. Their psychology experiments aiming to examine people's behavior led them to create the "prospect theory" (Kahneman and Tversky, 1979).

Based on their experiments, Kahneman and Tversky concluded that people value a positive benefit differently in monetary terms than they do a deprivation of the same benefit. This is in stark contrast to the axiom of *Homo economicus*, to which Neumann and von Morgenstern's theories of the behavior of a rational actor should apply (Neumann and von Morgenstern, 1944).

Kahneman and Tversky research subjects were introduced to games with either a positive or a negative prospect of success. They found that their subjects' preferences in games where the prospect was negative were mirroring their preferences in those with positive prospectuses. Changing the sign of the prospectus significantly changed the order of the subjects' preferences when making decisions. Kahneman and Tversky (1979) proved this by dividing the answers by the positive and negative prospectuses. They called their subjects' change in risk preference a "reflection effect."

To provide an example of their methodology: When a win was in principle possible, but unlikely, people chose to play a game with a potentially larger prize. If the same game were offered, but with negative prospects of winning, their preferences were the mirror image of their preferences in games with positive prospects. This outcome was inconsistent with the assumption that the subjects would choose rationally, as dictated by the *Homo economicus* axiom. Thus, prospect theory was a way to deal with the discovery of a "Kuhn anomaly," a violation of paradigm-induced expectations, during scientific research. Prospect theory does not entirely dismiss the idea of *Homo economicus*, but it does cast doubt upon its absolute validity. The fact that we can reach different conclusions by applying different theories to an economic phenomenon reflects the new spirit of science as defined by Bachelard (1999). The new scientific picture of the world is based on a neorealistic way of thinking. The absolutes of science are replaced by relative, probabilistic statements. Absolute theorems are no longer universally valid. A new scientific truth is born, a truth reflected in relative statements. Classical rationality falls apart and new rationality arises, its content being an epistemological revolution directed against Cartesian methodology and Bacon's inductive reasoning. One result is the new paradigm or process of interpretation known as behavioral economics, of which prospect theory is a part of (Kahneman and Tversky, 1979).

2.2 The Phenomenon of the Nudge

The nudge (Thaler and Sunstein, 2008) is a relatively new concept that is emerging in contemporary economic theory. It originates in behavioral economics (Twersky and Kahneman, 1974, 1981; Cartwright, 2011; Camerer and Loewenstein, 2004; Dolan et al., 2010). Its subject of research is the same as that of Descartes and Mises: human behavior. Behavioral economics attempts to understand economic behavior and its consequences. It examines why people make good and bad decisions and tries to help them make better decisions (Cartwright, 2011, p. 3). At the same time, it takes an oppositional stance towards the rational choice theory. Behavioral economics tests the standard economic models on real people and monitors whether they work. If they do not, it attempts to find ways to improve or change them to fit the observations better (Cartwright, 2011, p. 4).

In a research based on experimental data, behavioral economists start with existing economic models and identify violations of their assumptions. These violations can result from cognitive bias (Cialdini, 2008; Kahneman, 2011) or from other factors which may be social (Mazar and Ariely, 2006), emotional (Wilson and Gilbert, 2003; Loewenstein, Weber, Hsee, and Welch, 2001), psychological (Slovic, 1995; Kahneman, Knetsch, and Thaler 1991), or normative (Falk, 2007; Gouldner, 1960). The identified deviations from the expected outcomes lead to a new, alternative theory or an addition or formulation of a new model (Camerer; Loewenstein, 2004). This way, prospect theory was born. It is the basis of the nudge concept.

Kahneman and Tversky's prospect theory challenges the hypotheses of "expected utility" models in making choices between the present and the future under conditions of uncertainty. It draws attention to a number of outcomes that defy the postulates of the classical economic theory of rational choice (independence of consumer preferences as the initial state, completeness, independence of the presented order, transitivity, and higher utility at higher total consumption; Slovic, 1995). People act according to whether they perceive a given choice as leading to profit or loss (Plous, 1993). They tend to take risks when outcomes are likely positive and avoid risks when they are not (Tversky and Kahneman, 1981). Human behavior also tends to be inertial (status quo bias; Kahneman, Knetsch, and Thaler, 1991), supporting a libertarian paternalism based on the assumption that an appropriate offer of decision options (nudges) can produce desired results without excessively restricting people's freedom to decide for themselves (Thaler, 2015). Nudges are conscious changes to the institutional conditions of choice. They may promote healthier food choices, reducing the health and social care costs of obesity. The methodology may include simplifying information and choices, pre-defining choices, making healthy food more visible in supermarkets and canteens, pledges to oneself to meet specific goals, and other elements of a purposeful architecture applied in a physical or virtual context, like "traffic light labeling" (Reisch, Sunstein, and Gwozdz, 2016). We refer to these activities as "nudging." Oliver (2011) defines the catalytic role of the nudge as follows: Nudging brings different results to public policy. Some policies may prove effective, and others may not; furthermore, some policies prove effective but may be deemed politically or ethically unacceptable. This approach, however, involves no compulsion: people are free to get engaged in the change if they wish to do so but are not required to alter their behavior if they do not. (p. 1)

Nudge theory explores how to positively influence the behavior and decisions of various actors when they are hesitant to decide. A nudge can affect human behavior. It can have far-reaching societal implications, as shown by studies on health policy (Reisch, Sunstein, and Gwozdz, 2016). Society often struggles to positively influence health habits of individuals, such as their diets, and to motivate citizens to comply with preventive measures such as vaccinations (Maltz and Sarid, 2020). These are urgent social problems; it is therefore not surprising to see an increase in articles on this topic published in scientific journals.

2.3 Nudging Tools in Prospect Theory

In this chapter, we will examine nudging in scientific discourse. We used the Web of Science and Scopus databases of journals from 2017 to 2021. Our focus was on health policy. The phrase was chosen as the keyword for database searches. This phrase has broader meaning than the word "nudging." Initially, we wanted to capture a wide range of references in publications. We chose health policy as the research topic because nudging has the greatest potential for inducing change in this area bringing significant societal benefits. Thaler and Sunstein point to the usefulness and moral legitimacy of nudging in the area of health (Thaler and Sunstein, 2009). According to them, nudges are acceptable practice because they benefit the individuals exposed to them. Nudging has a positive impact on society as a whole as well. A nudge involves no obligation on the part of the targeted individual. It changes a person's behavior in a predictable way, but at the same time forbids nothing, nor does it force the nudged individual to do something. On the contrary, anyone is free to ignore a nudge, following them is not mandatory. Although we place the fruit in front of the consumer, we do not force them to consume it. Simply forbidding junk food would not be nudging, but coercion (Thaler and Sunstein, 2009). There is a fundamental difference between a restriction and a nudge.

Nudges can be classified in different ways depending on the distinguishing criteria used. Cadario and Chandon (2018) classify nudges as (1) cognitively oriented, such as descriptive or evaluative nutritional labeling and visibility enhancements; (2) affectively oriented, based on emotional appeals and not on data and logical argument; and (3) behaviorally oriented. They summarized these categories in a review article describing the influences that affect human behavior (Dolan et al., 2011). Dolan later developed a checklist of influences, calling it the mnemonic MINDSPACE (Dolan et al., 2018).

Table 1: The MINDSPACE

Messenger	We are heavily influenced by who communicates information.
Incentives	Our responses to incentives are shaped by predictable mental shortcuts, such as strongly avoiding losses.
Norms	We are strongly influenced by what others do.
Defaults	We "go with the flow" of pre-set options.
Salience	Our attention is drawn to what is novel and seems relevant to us.
Priming	Our acts are often influenced by subconscious cues.
Affect	Our emotional associations can powerfully shape our actions.
Commitments	We seek to be consistent with our public promises and reciprocate acts.
Ego	We act in ways that make us feel better about ourselves.

Source: Dolan et al., 2010

Halpern later modified the MINDSPACE checklist into the EAST framework, which adds the dimension of the timing of interventions (see Table 2).

Table 2: The EAST framework

Easy	People are more likely to do something if it's easy.
Attract	People are drawn to something that attracts their attention.
Social	People are strongly influenced by what other people do or have done.
Timely	Interventions are more likely to be effective if they happen before habits have formed.

Source: Halpern, 2016

According to the postulates of classical economics, consumer preferences are independent of the initial state, complete, independent of the order presented, and transitive. A larger number of offered goods should always bring a higher total benefit (Slovic, 1995). However, the research the behavioral economics is based on comes to a different conclusion about consumer preferences. It turns out that the Cartesian theoretical framework cannot explain why and how human behavior responds to nudging.

Kahneman (2011) came up with a dual theoretical framework of thinking systems (System 1 and System 2). This dual approach makes it possible to explain why our actual judgments and decisions often do not correspond to those that would be deemed rational. System 1 thinking is fast, automatic, intuitive, and is based on experience and emotions. It includes the innate mental capacities we are born with, such as the ability to perceive the world around us, to recognize objects, to focus our attention, and to avoid losses. Other mental abilities speed up and become automatic with long-term use.

System 2 thinking is slower, more reflexive, and more analytical. It is dominated by reason. System 2 thinking is usually activated when we attempt to do something that does not come naturally and requires some conscious mental strain. System 1 responds to heuristics (i.e., our cognitive biases) and is responsible for systematic distortions in decision making (Kahneman, 2011). The most universal cognitive phenomena are availability, affection, significance, status quo, inertia, optimism, overconfidence, distortion, and empathy. Availability and affection are internal phenomena. Availability is evident in a situation where investing for retirement may seem too risky because of the memory of a family member who lost most of their retirement savings in the recent recession (Tversky and Kahneman, 1974). The role of affection is evident in situations of uncertainty where an individual's emotional response to risk often differs from his or her cognitive assessment of the risk (Loewenstein, Weber, Hsee, and Welch, 2001).

Salience is an external process. Information that is new or which seems highly relevant is more likely than not to affect our thinking and actions (Dolan et al., 2010).

Using diet as an example, nutrition labeling on products can generate salience (Maheswaran, Mackie, and Chaiken, 1992). Maheswaran et al. found a relationship between purchasing behavior and the font size on the price tag. A discounted price in a smaller font led to a higher probability of purchase than when the price was presented in a relatively large font (Coulter and Coulter, 2005).

Consumer behavior can be influenced by rearranging the physical environment. For example, a nudge like moving bottled water closer to the cash register has been shown to significantly increase sales (Thorndike, Sonnenberg, Riis, Barraclough, and Levy, 2012).

People prefer compromise to a one-sided message. Humans prefer to maintain the status quo unless there is strong motivation to do otherwise. (Kahneman, Knetsch, and Thaler 1991). Inertia, procrastination, and lack of self-control are personality traits that argue for changing the default behavior from "opt-in" to "opt-out" to get the desired result. Madrian and Shea (2001) documented a significant change in the participation of employees in the retirement scheme of a large US corporation before and after a transition to automatic registration (i.e., a change from "opt-in" to "opt-out" of the system). An initial contribution percentage and investment allocation were set by the company (the "choice architect") and changing them required an affirmative act by the employee. Employee participation in the system was significantly higher with automatic registration ("opt-out"). This result has major implications for health policy. According to Johnson and Goldstein (2004), people are more likely to donate organs when they are required to opt out of donating than when they are required to opt in.

Research by Hershfield, et al. has suggested that behavioral change can be achieved by helping people to connect with their future selves using virtual reality (computer simulations). In all cases, participants in the study showed a preference for future cash returns over immediate ones. (Hershfield et al., 2011). This finding can be applied to create a health nudge for preventing civilization diseases.

People often overestimate the probability of future positive events and underestimate the probability of future negative events (Sharot, 2011). For example, we underestimate the risk of disease and overestimate our future success in healing. Overconfidence means that a person's subjective confidence in their own abilities is greater than their objective actual performance (Pallier et al., 2002). Excessive risk-taking has been observed among investors (e.g., Hirshleifer and Luo, 2001) in terms of maintaining highly concentrated portfolios (e.g., Odean, 1998) and too-frequent trading (e.g., Grinblatt and Keloharju, 2009). According to Kahneman, excessive trust may be the most significant of all cognitive prejudices (Kahneman, 2011, p. 129). When we plan for the future, we are often too optimistic. For example, we often underestimate how long it will take us to complete a task and ignore our past experience to the contrary (Kahneman, 2011).

Time discounting theory suggests that current events carry more weight in our calculations than future events (Frederick, Loewenstein and O'Donoghue, 2002). Our present selves cannot accurately predict the preferences of our future selves. This is called a diversification distortion (Read and Loewenstein, 1995). The bias against the future is especially strong if we go food shopping right after we have eaten.

Loewenstein called the inability to fully evaluate the effect of emotional and physiological stress on decision-making the "hot-cold empathy gap." Hot feelings include negative emotions associated with high levels of arousal (e.g., anger and fear) due to pain, hunger, thirst, addiction, or sexual arousal (Loewenstein, 2000). Men in a "cold" state of emotion are often sure they will use a condom in their next sexual intercourse, but when they are in an excited "hot state," they do not (Ariely and Loewenstein, 2006). In our predictions of our future feelings, we may overestimate how intense our emotions will be (Wilson and Gilbert, 2003).

The theory of hedonic adaptation suggests that changes in our life tend to evoke temporary feelings of happiness as we become accustomed to new circumstances (Frederick and Loewenstein, 1999). Although neoclassical economic theory argues that trusting strangers is irrational, relations of trust and credibility are commonly observed in all societies. Trust is associated with an aversion to betrayal. People are more willing to risk on a loss than on being deceived by another person, even when the probabilities are the same (Bohnet, Greig, Herrmann, and Zeckhauser, 2008). In addition, it has been found that individuals or institutions with high social status (e.g., physicians, teachers, the media, and government) have greater credibility than those with lower status. They can nudge citizens towards a healthy lifestyle more easily (Glaeser et al., 2000). For example, reminders sent by the UK's National Health Service in the form of cell phone text messages have improved participation in cervical cancer screening in Britain (Huf et al., 2020).

Data on people's interest in physical activity collected before and during the COVID-19 pandemic in Australia, the United Kingdom, and the United States during the twelve-month period from May 26, 2019, to May 22, 2020, show that their interest in exercise increased sharply immediately after fitness centers were closed down. Their interest peaked in the first two weeks, then declined, but still remained at a higher level than before the closures.

Increased health awareness and ubiquitous recommendations for exercise during the pandemic coming from the media, governments, and health authorities (including the WHO) encouraged people to adopt an active lifestyle (Ding et al., 2020). People typically value honesty, have a strong belief in morality, and want to maintain an honest and moral self-image (Mazar et al., 2008).

Social norms are typically defined as "rules and standards that are understood by members of a group, and that guide or constrain social behaviors without the force of law" (Cialdini and Trost, 1998, p. 152). Crossman (2021) distinguishes four key types of norms, with differing levels of scope and reach, significance and importance, and methods of enforcement. These norms, in an increasing order of significance include folkways, mores, taboos, and laws. Folkways (e.g., the concept of dressing appropriately, the practice of raising one's hand to take turns speaking in a group) are "norms that stem from and organize casual interactions and emerge out of repetition and routines" (Sumner, 1906). We engage in them to satisfy our daily needs. Mores (e.g., religious doctrines) structure the difference between right and wrong. Taboos (e.g., eating pork in some Muslim cultures) are a very strong negative norm; it is a prohibition of certain behavior that is so strict that violating it results in extreme disgust and even expulsion from the group or society (Crossman, 2021). Laws are norms that are issued and enforced by state authorities. Black (1972) views law as "a social control (the regulation over the actions of individuals and groups) by government." Social norms signal appropriate behavior for most people. Positive feedback for compliance with norms is often used in behavioral change programs along with informational feedback (e.g., informing people about how much money they have saved by not drinking, or by not neglecting medical and pharmaceutical care) (Diclemente et al., 2001). Nonprofits sometimes use information about norms to influence the amount of donations they receive. When potential donors were provided with information signaling the existence of a social norm (e.g., "We had a donor who contributed $300."), an average 12% increase in contributions was observed (Shang and Croson, 2009). A breakdown of social norms encourages dishonest behavior by promising high returns with low costs (Mazar and Ariely, 2006). Charities sometimes use reciprocity ("both you and I benefit") to their advantage. When potential donors were sent a gift in advance of any contribution as an expression of gratitude, the frequency of charity donations increased by 75% (Falk, 2007). Gouldner (1960) described reciprocity as a "generalized moral norm" among human beings. Cognitive dissonance theory posits a human need for a continuous, consistent self-image (Cialdini, 2008). People best achieve consistency by making a commitment to a behavior, especially if it is done in public. Patients are less likely to miss a doctor's appointment if they make a written commitment to keep it or if they receive information about faithful participation by other patients. (Martin, Bassi, and Dunbar-Rees, 2012). The Save More Tomorrow program designed by economists Richard Thaler and Shlomo Benartzi, which aims to encourage employees save more money for their retirement, has been shown to increase contributions to defined-contribution pension plans (Thaler and Benartzi, 2004). The psychological phenomenon of inertia increases the likelihood that employees will continue to contribute because they must affirmatively opt out of the program.

Herd behavior is another obvious influence on people's actions. Banerjee (1992) illustrates herd behavior with historical examples of collective investor irrationality and stock market bubbles. Shiller (2015) pointed out that speculative bubbles, such as the "Dotcom" stock market bubble of the late 1990s and the real estate bubble of the first decade after 2000, are driven by infectious enthusiasm among investors and sharing of stories that justify stock price increases. People sometimes make mistakes because they behave like sheep, and at other times they make mistakes because they behave like mules. Investors tend to leave profitable positions too soon and hold on to losers too long (Novotný, 2018 according to Belsky and Gilovich, 2008).

The study of human behavior shows that people do not act the way the rationalist theory based on the *Homo economicus* axiom predicts. Prospect theory offers a satisfactory alternative explanation (Kahneman and Tversky, 1999). Experiments testing prospect theory have refuted the hypotheses of the traditional model of decision making in conditions of uncertainty and of choosing between present and future benefit. Prospect theory confirmed that perceived loss is more significant than equivalent gain and that a certain gain is preferred over a speculative gain. Our willingness to take risks depends on the context. It is therefore influenced by the way behavior options are formulated. Giving something up has greater, more painful emotional impact than the pleasurable feeling of receiving something. Aversion to loss forces us to control our consumption expenditures (Prelec and Loewenstein, 1998, p. 4). Tightwads have an especially great aversion to loss. As a result, they are more sensitive to price incentives than most people (Rick, 2018, p. 767).

In developing the prospect theory, Kahneman and Tversky (1979) identified the certainty effect in addition to aversion to loss (in decision making, when presented with the certainty of a gain people tend to avoid risk, but when presented with the certainty of a loss, they tend to take a risk). They also identified the isolation effect (to simplify decision making, people often ignore the common components of alternatives and focus only on the differences).

The framing effect results from the way the choices are presented to a person, affecting their preferences. People make different choices depending on whether they perceive the choice as a potential gain or loss, based on the arguments presenting it (Plous, 1993). If arguments are framed positively, they are more willing to take a risk. If they are framed negatively, they avoid risk (Tversky and Kahneman, 1981). One result of the framing effect is that consumers choose to buy more optional features of a product when it is framed as a removing the feature rather than adding it (Biswas, 2009). In another case, a positively framed presentation of nutritional information reduced the research subjects' calorie intake by approximately 5% (Gustafson and Zeballos, 2020).

Until now, efforts to induce changes in health behavior (e.g., smoking cessation) have been strictly limited to educating patients about economic costs and negative health consequences. Reach (2016) examined the differences between educational efforts and nudging. He concluded that patient education is not always as transparent and well-designed as might be expected.

In contrast, nudging (e.g., using smartphone apps to facilitate quitting smoking) provides positive feedback (framing) along with information on health improvement and disease prevention. (Diclemente et al., 2001). "People will protect themselves with sunscreen if their application focuses on the benefits (e.g., healthy, youthful-looking skin) rather than the risks (skin cancer, premature skin aging)" (Detweiler, Bedell, Salovey,

Pronin, and Rothman, 1999, pp. 189–196). "The use of electronic health records (EHR) has encouraged physicians to follow work procedures more rigorously" (Belli, 2020, pp. 3254–3261).

Mental accounting theory states that people treat money and assets differently, depending on factors such as their origin and intended use, instead of considering value in terms of profit or loss as in formal accounting. That is, they think in a relative way rather than in an absolute sense. (Thaler, 1999). People are willing to spend more money when they pay by credit card than when they pay in cash (Prelec and Simester, 2001). They are often unable to take full account of opportunity costs and fall into the trap of focusing on sunk costs. "We are more likely to spend a small inheritance and invest a big one" (Thaler, 1985).

The phenomenon of overchoice is another example of people's bounded rationality. Due to an excess of choice, our ability to make decisions is paralyzed. This is true in all areas of life, including health. Overchoice leads to misfortune (Schwartz, 2004), decision making fatigue, preference to take the first option presented, and also to postponement of making any choice at all such as a decision to buy a product or use a service. Chernev et al. (2015) identified four key factors (sample set complexity, decision task difficulty, preference uncertainty, and decision goal) that reliably and significantly mitigate the impact of excess choice. The effect of an excess of choice can be reduced by simplifying the selection criteria or the number of available options.

Thaler and Sunstein (2009) argue that experience, good information, and quick feedback are key factors that enable us to make the right decisions.

People sometimes deliberately choose not to take into account information or knowledge that is freely available. (Golman et al., 2017). Actively avoiding information, the so-called ostrich effect, has been documented by research which showed that investors were less likely to monitor their portfolios when the stock market was falling than when it was growing (Karlsson et al. 2009).

In healthcare, information avoidance is sometimes a strategic choice and can bring immediate benefits to people, in the short run, if it leads to avoiding negative consequences of said knowledge. Nevertheless, in the long run, it usually has negative utility because it deprives people of potentially useful information for decision making and feedback that guides future behavior. A serious example of the ostrich effect is when people do not come to collect the results of an HIV test (Sullivan et al., 2004).

Ariely (2008) introduced the zero-price effect, where consumer demand for a product increase if it is offered for free. The effect manifests itself even if only a part of a product is offered free of charge (e.g., "15% extra free," "no sugar"). Price is often perceived as an indicator of quality and can enhance the placebo effect in medical studies. Shiv, Carmon, and Ariely (2005) showed that the effects of a placebo were greater when expectations about the effectiveness of the supposed medicine were raised because of its high price (a process that seems to be unconscious). In several other experiments, the authors showed that consumers who paid a discounted price for a product (e.g., an energy drink) derived less benefit from its consumption (e.g., they were able to solve fewer quiz questions) than those who paid the normal price for it.

Ariely (2008) also conducted a psychological experiment showing the effect of an asymmetric choice (known as the decoy effect). Including an inferior option changes the decision-making process towards seeking an optimal solution. Inspired by a discounted subscription offer for The Economist (access to all of its web content for $59, print edition subscriptions for $125, or combined print and web subscriptions also for $125), Ariely found that including a seemingly inferior option (print edition subscription only) 84% of subscribers opted for the combined subscriptions and just 16% for web content only. When the print edition only option was omitted, only 32% of subscribers wanted the combined print and web subscription, while 68% preferred the web content only. The presence of an inferior option nudged the decision-making process towards a combined web and print subscription, which objectively is the optimal solution. Ariely described the same effect in a number of other situations, including travel decisions and even assessing physical attractiveness: "People seem to look more attractive when they are accompanied by a sibling who is similar to them but is uglier." (2008, pp. 144–169)

Choices are often made on the basis of what the given options are rather than on the basis of absolute preferences. In the context of health care, the decoy effect works as a nudge when a third (similar but less attractive) drug or vaccine option influences people's preference for one option over another. Maltz and Sarid (2020) found that this effect increased the rate of influenza vaccinations. People were offered the choice of being vaccinated either at the beginning of winter, which epidemiologists recommend, or at the end of winter. Vaccination at the beginning of winter was offered for free, unlike at the end of winter. This approach (offering a financial advantage for pre-season vaccination) encouraged participants to get vaccinated at the beginning of winter, which is known to be optimal.

Decisions also vary according to the point when alternatives are offered (anchoring effect). As the starting point changes, so do our decisions. "Children who eat meat as a first course are more likely to be overweight than children who eat vegetables at the beginning of a meal" (Tani et al., 2018, pp. 1–7). When nutrition labels (especially those in the form of traffic lights) are placed on the front of food packaging so that they are encountered right away when the purchase decision is being made, they are effective tools for raising consumer awareness of nutritional quality, which results in more frequent choice of healthy foods (Santos, 2020).

However, Seward and Soled (2019) argue that traffic-light labeling (green, yellow, and red indicators of healthy, neutral, and unhealthy food options) and changes to choose architecture (e.g., making healthy choices more convenient, for example by placing vegetables at the beginning of cafeteria serving lines) can promote healthy eating. However, they warn that traffic-light labeling can also lead to unintended consequences for people with a risk of eating disorders. Women with anorexia or bulimia ordered significantly fewer calories and women who tended to overeat ordered significantly more calories when offered traffic-light-labeled foods compared to those who were offered unlabeled foods (Haynos and Roberto 2017).

At the end of this chapter, allow us to show how the Fogg model for analyzing and designing human behavior (Fogg, 2009) addresses "triggering behaviors." The Fogg model speaks of triggers (facilitators and sparks). Fogg's model has been extended to include the role of signals by Caraban et al. (2019), who explain its elements as follows. "Facilitators" enhance desirable behaviors in people, "sparks" increase motivation, and "signals" indicate desirable behaviors. Sparks increase motivation by adjusting the perceived probability of loss, using placebos, supporting planning (public commitment), increasing accountability and personal control, offering attractive alternatives (such as decoys and misleading visualizations), and taking advantage of social acceptance mechanisms (e.g., social norms). Signals reinforce behavior by raising doubts, increasing discomfort with existing behavior, or by increasing preferences for certain stimuli (e.g., subliminal priming) (Caraban et al., 2019, pp. 1–12). The Fogg model provides a systemic functional explanation for human behavior based on the paradigm of prospect theory. It is also a tool for understanding and explaining how nudges work in the field of nutrition and health.

3. Food Nudges: Health Policy Tools in the Field of Bariatrics and Diabetology

3.1 Defining "Food Nudges"

Human behavior can be influenced in various ways. There are, for example, regulatory and law enforcement means. These include, for example, public policy instruments such as laws and government regulations. Public authorities have adopted regulations and procedures and used coercion to achieve desirable behavior in citizens. This is about influencing human behavior at the macro (society-wide) level. We can also influence human behavior on an individual level. Psychology calls this "persuasion" (Grác, 1985). Persuasion uses non-coercive tools to influence human behavior. The concept of the nudge brings a new perspective. We will now examine specifically "food nudging."

Food nudging is nudging used in the nutrition field. Public health officials have various tools to influence people's behavior which can take various forms.[2] Traditionally, the instruments include regulations and their enforcement (e.g., health-related laws and regulations and restaurant inspections). These instruments have the weight of government power behind them to ensure they are abided by. In addition to these

---

2   Hagmann et al. (2018) examined how the Swiss public accepted several government interventions (taxes, labels, and nudges) to reduce sugar intake. The interventions that were the least annoying (nutrition labeling on the front of product packaging that emphasized sugar content, and public health campaigns) received the most public support, while more restrictive interventions (such as taxation, substitution of sugar by artificial sweeteners, and reducing portion size) were accepted more reluctantly. In this context, Hausman and Welch (2010) pointed out that libertarian paternalism is in many cases not paternalistic at all. To a large extent, it is a rational systém of persuasion that systematically exploits the irrational factors that influence human decision making, but which thereby threatens individual freedom (regardless of how justified the intervention is).

tools, however, there are "non-coercive" tools. As regards such tools, public policy actors do not have, or do not choose to use, the coercive power at their disposal to force people to change their behavior. The literature most often discusses the use of such tools in regard to health and healthy eating. Such tools are generally well-accepted by the public.[3] One of the most important of them is nudging. Oliver (2013) considers nudging to be a nuanced approach to promoting of healthy eating, aiming to elicit voluntary changes towards desired behavior within the given institutional conditions of choice. We use the term "food nudges" for this in this book.

3.2 Methods and Methodology for Analyzing the Scientific Discourse in the Field of Food Nudges

In this part of the book, we will examine nudging for healthy eating (food nudges) in the field of diabetology as we encounter them in contemporary scientific discourse. We will examine selected peer-reviewed articles that have appeared in journals indexed in the Web of Science and Scopus databases for the period of 2017–21. As we analyzed the literature, we asked ourselves two basic research questions:

1. How has research focused on food nudges (i.e., nudges towards healthier food choices) developed in the last five years?
2. What are the opportunities for future research into food nudges?

Our method for reviewing the literature on food nudges is one introduced by Tranfield et al. (2003). They developed a system of classification for books and articles on "food nudges." The methodology used in this subchapter is also based on the review approach of Hohenstein et al. (2014). This approach considers time horizons, database selection, article selection, and article classification.

In our case, we proceeded as follows. The key word we used in our online database searches was "food nudges." Our search discovered 645 articles published between 2017 and 2021. We studied the abstracts and conclusions of each article to determine its relevance to our area of study. Irrelevant articles (e.g., publications about unhealthy habits

---

3   Reisch, Sunstein and Gwozdz (2016) showed strong support for "non-coercive" interventions in Europe: around 74% of the public in Italy, the UK and France, followed by 69% in Germany, 57% in Hungary, and 51% in Denmark.

unrelated to food, duplicates, review articles, and conference articles) were excluded. We focused on the studies what has been dealing with influencing behavior in relation to nutrition. Qualitative studies were excluded. Some of the studies we included examined both nudging and one or more other interventions (e.g., price-setting and tax interventions).

The result of the selection process was a sample of 147 articles (see diagram 1). We systematically structured those articles into twelve categories based on the interventions they discussed: labeling, salience, priming, proximity, defaults, social norms, monetary incentives, portion size nudges, positioning, decoys, framing, and combinations of them (multi-component nudges).

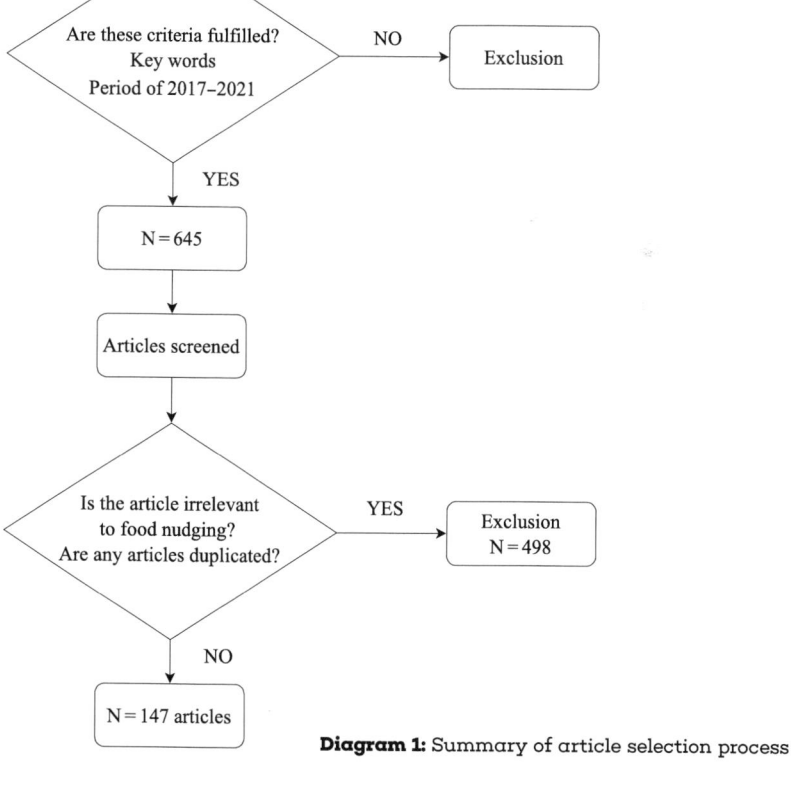

Diagram 1: Summary of article selection process

3.3 Results of the Analysis of Scientific Discourse: Identified Food Nudging Tools

Our analysis of the literature showed an increased level of interest in the issue of food nudges. When entering the keywords "food nudges" into the Web of Science database, the first record we found was from 1998 and the second record from 2004. Over the next nine years, only 11 articles were published. From 2013 to 2021 there was a clear increase in the number of published articles, especially since 2017. The following tables show the details.

Table 3: Identified Articles Relating to Food Nudging

Year	Web of Science	Scopus	Year	Web of Science	Scopus
2010	6	3	2016	33	22
2011	8	6	2017	52	35
2012	10	9	2018	70	37
2013	16	12	2019	83	47
2014	22	18	2020	88	52
2015	29	14	2021	102	79

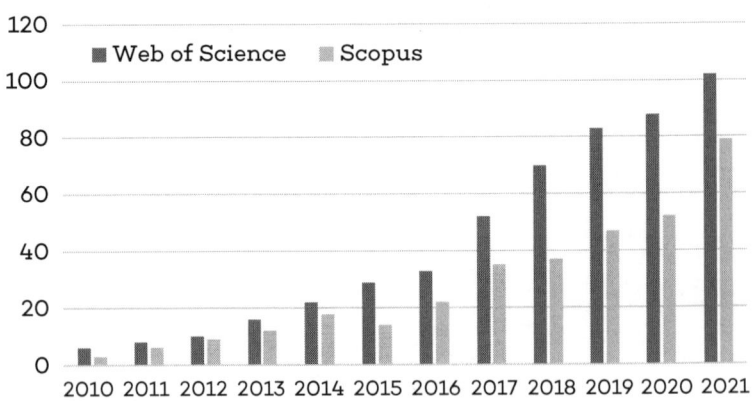

Graph 1: Search Results for the Keywords "Food Nudges"

Source: Web of Science and Scopus databases. Tables: authors.

The vast majority of the studies we included in our review confirmed the significant effect of nudges. Only 26 studies did not concluded there was a significant correlation between interventions and changes in respondents' behavior: Erjavec et al., 2020; Lai, List, and Samek, 2020; Kosīte et al., 2019; Zhou et al., 2019; Boehm et al., 2020; Attwood et al., 2020; Ohlhausen and Langen, 2020; Szakaly et al., 2020; Seward and Soled, 2020; dos Santos et al., 2018, 2020; Cheung et al., 2019; Reijnen et al., 2019; Thunstrom et al., 2018; Rogus, 2018; Stamos, 2018; Mors et al., 2018; Van Kleef et al., 2020; Wyse et al., 2019; Castellari et al., 2018; Immink et al., 2021; Hoenink et al., 2021; Magdaleno et al., 2021; Kraak et al., 2017; Stämpfli et al., 2017; and Ewert, 2017. In five studies, the research was conducted in more than one country (dos Santos et al., 2020; Peng-Li et al., 2020; Montagni et al., 2020; Cadario and Chandon, 2020; Zhou et al., 2019). Two studies did not specify the country (Coucke et al., 2019; Reinoso-Carvalho, F. et al., 2021). The peer-reviewed articles in our sample were published in a wide range of journals. For example, 28 articles were published in Appetite, 11 in Food Quality and Preference, six in Nutrients, and six in The International Journal of Behavioral Nutrition and Physical Activity. One-third of the articles were aimed at primary school pupils or secondary school students. These studies examined the impact of different kinds of interventions (e.g., labeling and product placement). Based on our analysis of the scientific discourse in this area, we identified the following types of food nudges.

Table 4: Typology of Food Nudges

Priming	Defaults
Labeling	Framing
Positioning	Monetary Nudges
Proximity	Salience Effect
Size Nudges	Social Norms
Decoy Effect	Multi-Component Nudges

In the following section, we will examine these types and some of the tools in each category in more detail.

3.3.1 Priming and Labeling

Most of the articles showed that strong arguments (Djupegot et al., 2019), having a purchaser set a calorie goal before shopping (Mohr et al., 2019), giving instructions at the moment food is consumed (Munoz-Vilches et al., 2019), exposure to informational placemats in a restaurant (Anzman-Frasca et al., 2018), improving the attractiveness of images accompanying healthy recipes (Starke et al., 2021), using contrasting colors (Wan et al., 2021), and claiming mental health benefits (Sogari, 2019) all had the potential to nudge people towards healthy eating choices. When consumers are primed to make environmentally friendly choices in their purchases, they are willing to pay more for such goods (Grebitus et al., 2020). A study by Bleasdale et al. (2021) confirmed that offering samples for tasting and otherwise prompting consumers at the point of purchase increased healthy food purchase from food trucks. Likewise, Villinger et al. (2021) showed that providing diners with a sugar shaker modified to restrict its flow can be an effective way to reduce the sugar added to hot beverages, without meeting with consumer disapproval. Trakman et al. (2021) concluded that a display that used traffic-light labeling was a low-cost, easy-to-implement strategy that can increase the consumption of healthy foods in community canteens. Social nudges rely on social influences, such as prompts of what the majority of people think, or a set phrase routinely said by a cafeteria staff member to diners. These have been found to be effective in changing behavior (e.g., Furth-Matzkin and Sunstein, 2018). Charry and Tessitore (2021) showed that the consumption of healthy food at social gatherings was inhibited by a perception of low social value. Its social value might be improved by nudges that communicate factors like a large number of people promoting the healthy food item on social media.

Mors et al. (2018) observed little or no effect of odor primes on food choices. Stamos et al. (2018) showed that priming healthy-weight individuals before meals is more effective than among obese people. Auditory impressions (Peng-Li et al., 2020) and visual impressions from prompts at the point of purchase (Allan and Powell, 2020), food imagery directed at the senses (Lange et al., 2020), better food presentation, improved availability of target foods, modifying the environment where food is consumed (Walker et al., 2019; McAlister et al., 2020; Erjavec et al., 2020; Carroll et al., 2018) and timing of the presentation of a food (Tonkin et al., 2019) all show a significant positive effect on the choice to consume healthy food. Filimonau et al. (2017) demonstrated that communicating the nutritional value of dishes and the provenance of their ingredients affects consumers' choices when dining out. Restaurateurs should therefore consider displaying such information on their menus whenever possible in order to promote more socially and environmentally beneficial food choices.

Sharps et al. (2019) found exposing young people to Instagram images of their peers' size portions high-energy-dense snacks and sugar-sweetened beverages decreased the portions size desired by young people. Results from a study by Tijssen et al. (2017) revealed that package coloring that identified "healthier alternatives" was associated with healthier items. Package coloring representing "regular products" was more strongly associated with attractive items. These results indicate that certain package color cues (i.e., bright colors, low color saturation) evoke associations with health, whereas other color cues (i.e., duller colors, high color saturation) evoke associations with attractiveness. These results are similar to those of Strugnell (1997). who demonstrated that red-colored drinks tended to be perceived as sweeter, while blue-colored drinks were evaluated as being less sweet.

Nudging by creating a vegetarian "Dish of the Day" increased sales of that dish. The impact of such a nudge was greater for less popular dishes. Its influence also increased when the number of food options presented to diners was increased (Saulais et al., 2019). However, in another study by Zhou, et al., the "Dish of the Day" nudge did not influence older people when choosing between veggie balls, meatballs, and fish cakes. However, participants from the UK and Denmark were more likely to choose a plant-based dish than those from France (Zhou et al., 2019). Grutzmacher et al. (2018) observed significant positive results when using text messages. Rogus (2018) examined the relationship between perceived and objective time constraints and the quality of Americans' food purchases by income level. In a different study, Erjavec et al. (2020) reported mixed outcomes that changes of the choice architecture in school canteens could increase the choice of fruit by schoolchildren, but their consumption of vegetables did not change, or even declined. On the other hand, Boehm et al. (2020) found no evidence that promoting healthy school meals reduced sales of less healthy foods. Adding health or taste messaging to packaging did not seem to make a difference in the consumption of healthier white milk relative to sugar-sweetened chocolate milk (Lai, List, and Samek, 2020). Blom et al. (2021) found that time pressure made no difference in the purchase of healthy nudged products. They also found that system 1 ("fast") thinking is not required for nudges to be effective in supporting healthier choices. According to Mai and Hoffmann (2017), the appearance of quality in a food does not assure its healthiness, but it does promote healthy food choices. Remarkably, the consumer's preference for quality and attractive physical appearance of food has even stronger effect on food choices than a personal preference for maintaining good health. Mai and Hoffman's article contributed to a shift in the prevailing paradigm by suggesting that healthier food consumption can be a side effect of higher quality and better appearance of food. It was their central premise that there are qualities of food that result in healthier nutrition behaviors even though they are not directly related to health considerations.

Filimonau and Krivcova (2017) argue that:

> Consumer choice ought to be architected to make it more responsible, thus facilitating progress of the hospitality industry in general, and its catering sector in particular, towards sustainability. Restaurants should play a more pro-active role in consumer choice architecture by "nudging" more benign purchasing decisions through menu design. The success of this "nudging" intervention depends on the managerial commitment (Filimonau and Krivcova, 2017, pp. 516–527).

Likewise, teaching cafeteria managers and staff members the Smarter Lunchrooms Movement techniques may be an effective way to make changes in school cafeterias to encourage healthier choices among students. Among adults with low socioeconomic position, the cost, convenience, healthiness, and taste, along with personal habits, were the most important determinants of food choice (Harbers et al., 2021). Food labeling that carries a positive nudge can contribute to healthy eating habits (Montagni et al., 2020; Benson et al., 2018, 2019; Cerezo-Prieto and Frutos-Esteban, 2021). The results of these studies indicate that health labels can be an effective signal and marketing tactic for nudging the parents of overweight or obese children toward healthier food purchases.

The visual appearance of packaging can also be used strategically for nudging consumers toward healthier purchase habits (Reinoso-Carvalho, 2021).

When consumers were presented with a visual scale running from "healthy" on the left to "unhealthy" on the right, they preferred low-calorie foods to high-calorie ones (Manippa et al., 2020). Similarly, Santos et al. (2020) found that traffic-light labeling received more favorable responses from consumers than guideline daily amounts (the ideal amounts of food components that a person should consume each day), Nutri-Scores (similar to traffic-light labeling), and health star ratings (labels that assign a greater number of stars to healthier foods). Providing calorie counts on restaurant menus to the left of listed food items (for those reading from left to right) decreased the total number of calories diners ordered (Dallas et al., 2019). Rising and Bol (2017) argue that positioning calorie information nudges next to menu items should result in diners choosing lower-calorie salad and beverage options. They found that a diner's feeling of self-control moderated the effect of calorie labeling on food choices. Specifically, diners who felt they had high self-control said that a calorie-label nudge influenced them to select a lower-calorie salad option. The authors did not see the same effect for beverages. Nevertheless, Policastro et al. (2017) found a calorie-labeling message very promising for motivating customers to choose water over sugar-sweetened beverages. Mecheva et. al (2021) found that exposing children to negative peer behavior (a peer choosing a sugary snack rather than a banana) had greater effect on their choice of snack than did positive peer behavior. They concluded that the direction of nudges displaying peer behavior is important to designing healthy eating interventions targeted at children.

On the other hand, Mazza et al. (2018) reported both positive and negative outcomes of traffic-light labeling interventions. Szakaly et al. found that their subjects perceived healthy samples of food (cheeses) with considerably less sensory pleasure than the less healthy ones. Food labeling may even have undesirable consequences for women with anorexia nervosa or bulimia nervosa (Seward and Soled, 2020). Bacon and Krpan (2018) argue that people's individual past behavior is an important determinant of the impact of food nudges and thus a personalized intervention is required in order to induce change. Similarly, Castellari et al. (2018) argue that menu labeling has only a small or even no effect by itself. They suggested that adding nutrition information alone to a restaurant menu does not necessarily encourage healthier choices by diners. Requiring nutritional labeling in a dining-out environment may be ineffective because of many unobservable or unrecorded factors, such as the characteristics of the restaurant environment, the wording of the label, the type of label, and the behavior of the diner. (Castellari et al., 2018). Last but not least, Hoenink et. al. (2021) indicated that placing labels on store shelves that indicated the sugar content of beverage products did not significantly change the composition of sales for four beverage categories (green, blue, yellow, and amber), nor was there a difference in total beverage sales revenue. From our analysis of studies dealing with the effects of priming and labeling nudges, we believe that both types of nudges can influence people's dietary decisions.

3.3.2 Positioning, Proximity, and Size Nudges

In this section, we will examine the influence of positioning, proximity, and size nudges.

Positioning. An Australian study achieved positive changes in food choices by using positioning nudges (Keegan et al., 2019). For example, participants in the study were significantly more likely to choose a salad when it was presented to them separately rather than on a plate along with unhealthier food options. Van Gestel et al. (2018) observed a positive effect of a nudge that involved repositioning a healthy food choice in a kiosk (closer to the checkout counter). Similarly, Mikkelsen et al. (2021) showed that rearranging beverages by placing healthier ones at eye-level had a positive effect on their sales. Vandenbroele et al. (2021) showed that offering a meat substitute next to a similar meat product in the butcher shop (instead of separately in a vegetarian section) created an effective choice architecture that significantly increased the sale of meat substitutes.

An Australian study conducted by Wyse et al. (2019) found that positioning target products first or last on the online menu of a canteen did not increase customers' choice of those items. However, a Swiss study supervised by Reijnen et al. (2019) confirmed that appetizers appearing at the top of a menu were chosen more often than other menu items. On menus offering the most preferred dishes, participants chose entrées appearing in the middle of the menu significantly more often. No positioning effect could be detected for desserts. Kim et al. (2019) found that items appearing in the middle of a menu are preferred when they are displayed horizontally, whereas items along the edge of the page were preferred on a vertical display.

Proximity. According to Ghoniem et al. (2020), the desire for food peaks when food is available at a moment of high need. It is a positive learning experience. An American study conducted by Knowles et al. (2019) revealed that the consumption of a target food item varied depending on the relative position of another item. To maximize healthy choices, supermarkets can move healthy items closer to the shopper and unhealthy items further away. Van Kleef et al. (2020) demonstrated that increasing the availability of healthier products in school canteens resulted in small positive changes in diner's behavior. Similarly, Immink et al. (2021) showed that offering healthy snacks in the workplace can be a valuable way to promote workers' health.

Size nudges. Reducing the size of food portions sizes may change diners' perceptions of what constitutes a "normal" amount of food to eat (Robinson and Kersbergen, 2018). Doubling the number of vegetarian meals available from 25% to 50% increased the sales of vegetarian meals and decreased the sales of meat-based dishes. (Garnett et al., 2019). Likewise, changing the size of the display area and the number of products displayed influenced the consumers' purchasing behavior (Coucke et al., 2019). Petit et al. (2018) employed the Delboeuf illusion (two discs of the same size appear different in size depending on whether they are surrounded by a larger or smaller ring) as a nudge to make food seem more desirable, while at the same time leading consumers to reduce how much they consumed. The effect of a portion size nudge was apparent among people who usually add a certain number of teaspoons of sugar to their tea (Venema et al., 2020). However, Kosīte et al. (2019) found that there was no evidence that the size of tableware has an effect on the amount of food consumed.

3.3.3 Decoy Effect, Default Options, Framing, Monetary Nudges, Salience Effect, and Social Norms

In addition to the types of food nudges mentioned above, other categories have been identified. These include the decoy effect, defaults, framing, monetary nudges, the salience effect, and social norms. From our analysis of the literature, we draw the following conclusions for these individual categories:

Decoy effect. A study by Attwood et al.'s (2020) did not show any effect of providing an asymmetric choice of options, that is, there was no decoy effect (e.g., a 30% increase in the price did not significantly change the number of people choosing an inferior "decoy" dish). Van den Enden and Geyskens (2021) suggest it would be effective to adjust the consumers' environment, so they are nudged towards buying a healthy product, rather than openly urging them to choose a healthy alternative item.

Default options. Consumer choices are often influenced by the default option presented to them (van Kleef et al., 2018). Consumers' preference for the status quo (Bergeron et al., 2019) and a consumer's lack of self-control (Marques et al., 2020) seem to make changes in a default option from "opt-in" to "opt-out" effective (Dalrymple et al., 2020). Automatically adding vegetables to existing meal choices (Holligan et al., 2019) as well as providing an appropriate default option in an online shopping cart (Coffino et al., 2020) resulted in the improved nutritional quality of consumers' purchases. Likewise, Hansen et. al (2021) showed that changing the default lunch offer to a vegetarian option was an effective, generic, easy to scale, and well-accepted nudge that promoted healthy, sustainable food choices at conferences.

Colby et al. (2020) suggest that "advertising" healthy default choices drives away future sales. This consumer "dodging effect" was significant in connection with a well-known brand.

Framing. Positive visual stimuli increased the probability that consumers would make a healthy snack choice (Benito-Ostolaza et al., 2021). At the same time, a combination of pro-environment, social, and neutral framings increased the likelihood consumers would buy a vegetarian choice compared to a strictly pro-vegetarian framing (Krpan and Houtsma, 2020). Both loss-framed and gain-framed messages influenced research subjects' perception of the safety of a food when the subjects had a low level of personal involvement with the issue of food safety. However, when they had a high level of personal involvement with the issue, their perceptions of a food's safety were influenced only by a loss-framed message. (Britwum and Yiannaka, 2019).

Monetary incentives. Cash rebates for customers who ordered vegetable-rich meals increased healthy food choices (Nagatomo, 2019). The proportion of vegetable-rich meal orders to meat-based dishes increased by 1.50 times (95% confidence interval [CI]: 1.29 to 1.75). The proportion of daily sales of vegetable-rich meals increased by 1.77 times (95% CI: 1.11 to 2.83), even considering the cost of the rebates. Based on the US National Household Food Acquisition and Purchase Survey (FoodAPS), which tracks individual's food purchases over one week, and using the Guiding Stars Program (GSP) algorithm to measure the nutritional quality of purchased food items, Zeballos, et al. (2020) observed that customers paying for their purchase in cash bought a larger share of healthy items than those who payed with a credit card. The research suggests that when people routinely use shopping lists, they tend to plan their grocery shopping more. This could result in fewer impulsive decisions compared to choosing foods in a setting away from home. This tendency may explain why we find that individuals who pay in cash do not purchase a larger share of items compared to those who use credit or debit cards. (Zeballos et al., 2020).

Salience. Positive results have been achieved by increasing the salience of nudges. Jinghui (2017) suggested that interface cues on a computer screen can function as nudges and influence consumers' decisions on a relatively autonomous level. Fennis et al. (2020) explored the impact of salient scarcity cues (e.g., "limited availability" and "while supplies last") and abundance cues (e.g., "all you can eat") upon consumers with fast and slow life history strategies. They found that consumers with slow life-history strategies were more susceptible to abundance cues, while those with fast strategies were prompted to make healthy choices by scarcity cues. Ozturk et al. (2020) found in their study that salient nudges were effective in promoting healthy food choices but that their impact was not long-lasting and disappeared when they were removed. At the same time, the effectiveness of interventions decreased with repetition. Thunström (2018) observed that both opportunity cost and spending booster reminders reduced spending by tightwads.

Social norms. Nudges that communicate social norms are a powerful tool for changing and promoting sustainable behavior with minimal associated costs. The studies we reviewed (e.g., Gonçalves et al., 2021) showed that it is possible to deploy such nudges in a retail context in order to change purchasing behavior. Participants in the study responded positively to social norm interventions. For example, a nudge on a card attached to shopping trolleys increased purchases of vegetables (Huitink et al., 2020). Exposing consumers to provincial norms, i.e., norms specific to the consumption of food, resulted in their making healthier consumption choices (Otto et al., 2019). Hogreve et al. (2020) demonstrated that a nudge based on social norms succeeded in influencing parents to choose a healthy food alternative for their children. The researchers' intervention increased parents' choosing of healthy food items by more than 29%. Similarly, according to Morren et al. (2021) the amount of information about sustainable or healthy diets that research subjects had was positively related to the sustainability of the participants' dietary choices. Hawkins et al. (2021) demonstrated that information received from social media can affect eating behavior by communicating social norms. Ewert (2017) argues that a settings approach focused on lifestyle, culture, and other social determinants of health is superior to nudges focused on individual choices, especially in schools. Griesoph et al. (2021) distinguished between "descriptive" and "guessed" norms:

While descriptive norms communicate typical patterns of behavior (e.g., 50% of canteen visitors choose vegetarian meals), guessed norms are determined by the individual's best guess about the norm in a specific context. The results confirmed a remarkable nudging effect of guessed norms: The higher the presumed proportion of vegetarian dishes sold, the lower the probability of choosing a vegetarian dish. Surprisingly, this effect is independent of the respective norm specification (meat or vegetarian norm).

3.3.4 Multi-Component Nudges

Most of the articles we reviewed combined various nudging interventions to influence food choices. For instance, Broers et al. (2019) effectively utilized title ("Suggestion of the Chef") and sample-tasting nudges. Fitzgerald et al. (2019) combined nutrition education and nudges delivered via smartphone. Hamdi et al. (2020) increased the selection of vegetables and fruit in school cafeterias using decorations, creative names for dishes, taste tests that created social norms, and "flavor stations" with spices and condiments. Mistura (2019) showed that the effect of product placement and sensory and cognitive nudges was greater among female purchasers than among male purchasers. Samek et al. (2019) found out that combining changes towards choice architecture, pledges to maintain healthy lifestyles, and material incentives increased the choice of healthier milk by 15% among schoolchildren. Giving the children the option to set their own goals increased the choice of healthy milk by 10%. The proximity effect appears to depend on the salience of visual cues, according to Knowles et al., 2020. Combining priming and social norms (Vermote et al., 2020) and physical cues and social norms (Raghoebar et al., 2019) led to increasing healthy food choices. In another study, combining three nudges (inducing cognitive fatigue, providing scarcity cues, and limiting the amount of product consumers were allowed to purchase) increased sales of promoted items. However, the researchers found no significant change when the nudges were implemented individually. (Chapman et al., 2019). Proximity, priming, and choosing an indulgent (high calorie) dish first in a cafeteria line may lower overall caloric intake. Flores et al. (2019) uncovered an interaction effect of food type (indulgent vs. healthy) and food presentation order (first vs. last) on individuals' subsequent food choices and their overall caloric intake. Friis et al. (2017) combined priming, default choices, and a perception of variety and found that a nudge can have different effects depending on whether it is aimed at increasing intake of healthy dishes or limiting the intake of unhealthy dishes. Their work demonstrated that consumer behavior can be influenced without restricting choice or providing incentives for behavior change.

Combining salient pricing and nudging strategies resulted in increases in the percentage of healthy products consumed regardless of the socio-economic position of the participants in the study by Hoenink et al., 2020. The results from two studies conducted in Africa emphasized the role of targeted and integrated nutrition education approaches in increasing the consumption of healthy sweet potatoes. (Just et al., 2021; Ojwang et al., 2021)

On the other hand, Cheung et al. (2019) recorded mixed outcomes from combined nudges. Making fruit accessible significantly increased its sales of it. However, the effectiveness of making it salient was limited, presumably by existing preferences or habits. Ohlhausen and Langen (2020) did not recommend a combination of labels and presenting a less attractive decoy dish next to a more attractive target dish in order to foster sustainable food choices. In that study, presenting a decoy dish had a negative influence on the participants' choice, probably because the consumers were not aware of the different sustainability ratings of the dishes, which were not indicated beside the dishes' names. The experts had not expected canteen guests to prefer the decoy dish, carrot lasagna, over the target dish, vegetable lasagna, which contained a larger variety of vegetables for the same price. In a 2017 meta-analysis of the literature on healthy eating nudges, Cadario and Chandon (2020) argued that interventions are more effective in reducing unhealthy eating than they are for increasing healthy eating or reducing total calories consumed. They found that the effects of nudges were more significant in the United States than in other countries, in restaurants, and cafeterias than in grocery stores, and in studies including a control group than in those that did not. The size of the effect of a nudge was found to be unrelated to the study duration and was similar for food selection versus food consumption and for both children and adults. Dos Santos et al. (2020) found that the use of a food choice questionnaire, social norm information, and a pre-existing favorable attitude towards vegetables were positively associated with the choice of a vegetable-based dish. Being male was negatively associated with choosing a vegetable-based dish.

According to Marcano-Olivier et al. (2019), positioning and labeling nudges resulted in increased consumption of fruit, vitamin C, and fiber. However, they recorded no changes in the consumption of vegetables.

Reynolds et al. (2019) demonstrated that labeling is the most acceptable nudge for consumers, followed by size, tax, and availability.

If we monitor how frequently the various types of nudges appear in the literature we reviewed, the situation is as follows (see Table 5).

Table 5: Distribution of Categories of Nudges in Reviewed Articles

Nudges	Number of Articles
Defaults	10
Decoy effect	2
Framing effect	3
Labeling	19
Monetary nudges	2
Multi-component nudges	33
Positioning	7
Priming	45
Proximity effect	5
Salience effect	4
Size effect	9
Social norms	8
Total	**147**

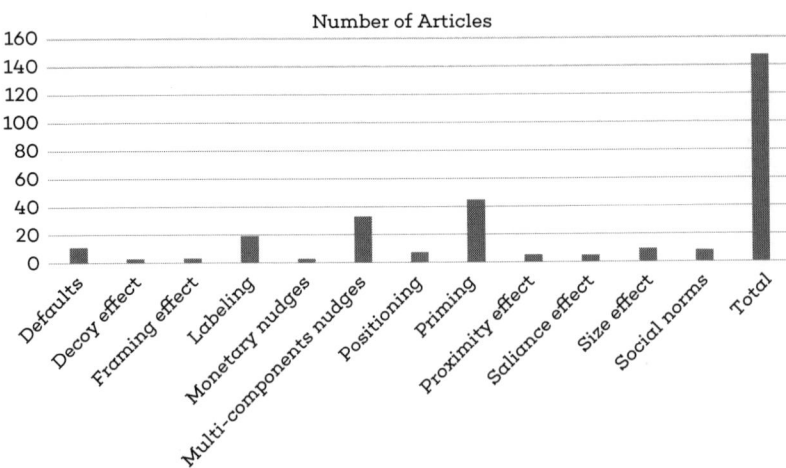

Graph 2: Distribution of Categories of Nudges in Reviewed Articles

4. Literature Review of Scientific Articles on Food Nudges

4.1 Country of Origin of Selected Scientific Studies

Most of the scientific articles we reviewed originated in a specific national context. The United States was by far the country with most research (40 articles). The United Kingdom and the Netherlands contributed with 22 and 18 articles, respectively. Three studies were conducted in several European countries (Denmark, France, Italy, the United Kingdom, Belgium, and France), two were conducted in both the US and France, and one in China and Denmark.

Only one study was conducted in one of the post-communist countries of Central and Eastern Europe, in Hungary. In Africa, studies on ways to promote the consumption of orange-fleshed sweet potatoes were conducted in Kenya and Nigeria.

Table 6: Country of Origin of Reviewed Articles

Country	Number of Articles
Australia	5
Belgium	5
Belgium, Greece	1
Canada	3
China	2
Denmark	5
Denmark, France, Italy, and the United Kingdom	2
Finland	1
France	3

France, United States	2
Germany	12
Hungary	1
China, Denmark	1
Indonesia	1
Ireland	3
Italy	2
Japan	1
Kenya	1
Netherlands	23
New Zealand	1
Nigeria	1
Norway	2
Portugal	2
Spain	2
Sweden	2
Switzerland	2
United Kingdom	18
United States of America	40
Not specified	3
Total	**147**

It is clear from our analysis that research on food nudges is distributed very unevenly in terms of the studies' country of origin. Research in the former Eastern Bloc countries lags far behind Western countries.

4.2 Classification of Analyzed Scientific Studies by Journals

In this section, we will examine the scientific journals where the articles we reviewed were published. We reviewed 139 scientific articles from a total of 75 journals. One-fifth of the articles was published in Appetite. The journals featuring the articles and the countries the research was conducted in are listed in Table 7 below.

Table 7: Journals in which the Reviewed Articles Appeared

Journal	Frequency	Country of Research	Nudge Category
Appetite	28	Australia, Belgium, France, Germany, Italy, Netherlands, Portugal, United Kingdom, United States	Decoy effect, Defaults, Labeling, Multi-component nudges, Priming, Proximity, Size nudges, Social norms
Food Quality and Preference	11	Belgium, Canada, China, Denmark, France, Germany, Italy, Netherlands, United Kingdom	Defaults Positioning, Priming, Salience
Nutrients	6	Canada, Denmark, Ireland, Switzerland, United States	Defaults, Labeling, Multi-component nudges, Priming
International Journal of Behavioral Nutrition and Physical Activity	6	Japan, Netherlands, United Kingdom	Monetary nudges, Priming, Multi-component nudges, Size nudges
Foods	3	Germany, Hungary, Unspecified country	Labeling, Multi-component nudges, Size nudges
Public Health Nutrition	3	Netherlands, United States	Multi-component nudges, Priming
American Journal of Clinical Nutrition	3	Australia, United Kingdom	Positioning, Size nudges
British Food Journal	2	Norway, United States	Defaults, Priming
Food Policy	2	France, United States	Priming, Monetary nudges
Journal of Economic Behavior and Organization	2	United States	Multi-component nudges, Salience
Nutrition Journal	2	Belgium, Netherlands	Multi-component nudges, Size nudges
Social Science and Medicine	4	United Kingdom, United States, Spain	Multi-component nudges, Priming
Frontiers in Psychology	2	Belgium, Netherlands	Priming, Proximity

International Journal of Consumer Studies	2	Denmark	Defaults, Priming
PLOS ONE	3	Netherlands, Denmark, United States	Multi-component nudges, Decoy effect
Sustainability	3	Portugal, Germany	Social norms
International Journal of Environmental Research and Public Health	6	Germany, Netherlands, United States, Australia	Priming, Proximity, Multi-component nudges
Others[4]	64	Australia, Belgium, Canada, China, Denmark, France, Germany, Ireland, Italy, Kenya, Netherlands, New Zealand, Nigeria, Norway, Spain, Sweden, Switzerland, United Kingdom, United States, Unspecified country	Defaults Framing Labeling Multi-component nudges Positioning Priming Salience Size nudges Social norms
Total	**147**		

---

4   The scientific journals include: *American Journal of Agricultural Economics, BMC Public Health, BMC Nutrition, Cornell Hospitality Quarterly, Digital Health, Eating Behaviors, European Journal of Clinical Nutrition, European Journal of Nutrition, Health Communication, Journal of American College Health, Journal of Behavioral and Experimental Economics, Journal of Business Research, Journal of Consumer Affairs, Journal of Consumer Policy, Journal of Consumer Psychology, Journal of Environmental Psychology, Journal of Epidemiology and Community Health, Journal of Experimental Psychology-Applied, Journal of Occupational and Environmental Medicine, Marketing Science, Proceedings of the National Academy of Sciences of the United States of America, Royal Society Open Science, Health Promotion Practice, Marketing Letters Ernahrungs Umschau, Physiology and Behavior, Journal of Hunger and Environmental Nutrition, Psychology and Health, Bio-Based and Applied Economics, Organizational Behavior and Human Decision Processes, Journal of Cleaner Production, Journal of Retailing, Frontiers in Sustainable Food Systems, Journal of Environmental Economics and Management, Journal of Computer-Mediated Communication, Journal of Cleaner Production, Social Theory Health, The International Review of Retail, Distribution and Consumer Research, Journal of Cleaner Production, Health Communication, Obesity, Agribusiness, Public Health Reports, Journal of Health Economics, Games, The American Journal of Clinical Nutrition, Journal of Environmental Psychology, Journal of American College Health, Public Health Nutrition, Organizational Behavior and Human Decision Processes, Frontiers in Psychology, International Journal of Workplace Health Management, Journal of Medical Internet Research, The European Journal of Development Research, Current Developments in Nutrition, Journal of Sensory Studies, Atención Primaria, Journal of Public Health (Oxford, England), Frontiers in artificial intelligence,* and *Applied Psychology: Health and Well-Being.*

There are differences in the approaches these journals take to the subject of health nudges. However, the differences result mainly from the different professional focuses of the journals. It is not surprising that one-fifth of the articles we reviewed were published in the journal Appetite, whose main focus is on the behavior of humans and animals toward food.

4.3 Detailed Results of the Literary Search by Category Nudges (Years of 2017–2021)

This chapter contains the detailed results of our review of the selected articles. For clarity, we have compiled the results into a table that provides information about the author(s) of the article, the year of publication, journal where it was published, data on the research methodology, key findings, and the type of nudge(s) studied. The articles we reviewed were published between 2017 and 2021. We did the "donkey work" of searching for the individual articles and analyzing their content. The output of our analysis, as presented in the following extensive table, not only provides an overview of the current literature, but also provides information useful in further scientific research to all researchers and interested parties, saving them significant effort.

Table 8: Results of Literature Search of Articles Published from 2017 to 2021, Sorted by type of the Nudge

Authors, Year, Journal, Country	Participants
Attwood, S. et al. 2020 Appetite United Kingdom	N^i = 147 N^{ii} = 472 University students
van den Enden, G. and Geyskens K. 2021 PLOS ONE Netherlands	N = 237 (76.4% female, Mage = 35.5) 2 (attraction effect manipulation: no-decoy or decoy) ×3 (type of choice set: unhealthy, healthy, and mixed) design was applied.
Hansen, P. G., Schilling, M. and Malthesen, M. S. 2021 Journal of Public Health (Oxford, England) Denmark	N^i = 170, N^{ii} = 174, N^{iii} = 130 Participants of 3 conferences were randomized into two groups: Group 1 received a standard lunch registration offering a non-vegetarian buffet as the default but allowing the active choice of a vegetarian option; Group 2 received a registration presenting a vegetarian buffet as the default, allowing the active choice of a non-vegetarian option. The study also assessed gender differences for two of the conferences and the participants' acceptance of the nudge at one of the conferences.
Holligan, S. et al. 2019 British Food Journal United States	N = 686 University students
Marques, I. C. F. et al. 2020 Nutrients Denmark	N = 83 University students (84%)
Coffino, J. A. et al. 2020 Appetite United States	N = 50 Recruits from Food Pantries

Focus area	Key Findings
Decoy effect	Price-based decoy strategy (a 30% price increase) did not significantly influence the number of people choosing the inferior decoy dish. (Salad vs. burger menu p = 0.31; salad vs. curry menu p = 0.35; salad vs. brunch menu p = 0.33)
Decoy effect	Adding a decoy enabled consumers to make healthier food choices. The relative portion of the target was higher with the decoy condition (76.0%) than in the no-decoy condition (52.5%; β = 1.113, χ^2 (1) = 11.85, p = 0.001, Nagelkerke R2 = 0.216).
Defaults This study investigates a simple, generic, and easily scalable nudge to promote healthy and sustainable food choices at conferences by using a vegetarian lunch-default as a normative signal.	In the experiment A the vegetarian choice increased from 2% to 87% (N = 108, p < 0.001). In experiment B it increased from 6% to 86% (N = 112, p < 0.001). In experiment C it increased from 12.5% to 89% (N = 110, p < 0.001). A significant tendency for men, but not women, to opt out of the vegetarian default was found. A clear majority of participants reported positive attitudes toward the nudge.
Defaults	More vegetables incorporated into existing composite meals were offered as the new default in university cafeterias. Broccoli was the most preferred vegetable for sit-down meals. For portable meals (sandwiches, pitas, and wraps), preferred vegetables for modification were cucumbers, spinach, tomatoes, and bell peppers.
Defaults	Nudging works independently of the impulsivity score. Individuals with lower self-control may benefit more from certain nudging interventions. Impulsivity scores of the sample population showed higher scores in the "sensation seeking" trait (mean = 2.8) and lower impulsive scores in the "lack of premeditation" trait (mean = 1.8).
Defaults	A default option of an online shopping cart appears to improve nutritional quality of food purchases. Compared to nutrition education, the default shopping cart resulted in the purchase of significantly more ounces of whole grains (Mean Difference [Mdiff] = -4.05; 95% Confidence Interval [CI] = -6.14, -1.96; p < 0.001), cups of fruits (Mdiff = -1.51; 95% CI = -2.51, -0.59; p = 0.002) and vegetables (Mdiff = -2.21; 95% CI = -4.01, -0.41; p = 0.02), foods higher in fiber (mg; Mdiff = -15.65; 95% CI = -27.43, -3.87; p = 0.01), and lower in sodium (mg; Mdiff = 1642.66; 95% CI = 660.85, 2624.48; p = 0.002), cholesterol (mg; Mdiff = 463.86; 95% CI = 198.76, 728.96; p = 0.001), and grams of fat (Mdiff = 75.42; 95% CI = 42.81, 108.03; p < 0.001) and saturated fat (Mdiff = 26.20; 95% CI = 14.07, 38.34; p < 0.001).

Authors, Year, Journal, Country	Participants
Dalrymple, J. C. et al. 2020 Appetite United States	Data analysis in two restaurants (Children and/or parents)
Bergeron, S. et al. 2019 Food Quality and Preference Canada	N = 303 (Age range of 45 to 53)
van Kleef, E. 2018 Appetite Netherlands	N = 226 (University students)
Colby, H. et al. 2020 Organizational Behavior and Human Decision Processes United States	N = 1002 (5 studies were conducted in a university store)
Torma, G. et al. 2018 International Journal of Consumer Studies Denmark	N = 10 (Aarhus university employees)

Focus area	Key Findings
Defaults	Positioning lower-energy-dense foods as default menu choices increased the likelihood their being selected and decreased the likelihood that customers would "opt-out." During the Optimal Default Menu condition, 49.8% of selections were lower-energy-dense, compared to 15.4% of selections from the Suboptimal Default Menu condition and 27.0% from the Free Array Menu condition in Restaurant A. Lower-energy-dense selections comprised of 42.2% selections made during the Optimal Default Menu condition, compared to 6.1% for the Suboptimal Default Menu condition and 18.1% for the Free Array Menu condition in Restaurant B.
Defaults	Status Quo bias can be used to nudge towards healthier choices on menus. Automatic and standard defaults affected choices but did not adversely impact the satisfaction of individual choices. When the standard was a richer version, this corresponded to choosing the alternative, but when the standard was a lighter version, it corresponded to choosing the standard. 38% of participants choose the alternative presented as "lower in version of the dessert. This choice decreased to 31% when the standard default was presented the automatic choice. 25% of the participants choose the alternative presented as "enriched in version of the dessert." That percentage was reduced to 14% when the standard was presented as the automatic choice. The selection of the alternative significantly increases when it is set as the default choice. In fact, the number of participants selecting the lighter version of the dessert when presented as the alternative increased from 38% to 79% when it was set as the automatic choice. The number of participants who selected the alternative enriched version of the dessert increased from 25% in the neutral treatment to 67% when it was set as the automatic choice.
Defaults	When the whole wheat bun was offered to choose, 108 out of 115 participants (94%) decided to stick with the default option. Similarly, when the white bread was offered as the default option, 89 out of 111 participants (80%) chose this.
Defaults	Consumers dodge healthy defaults by migrating to environments where unhealthy defaults are in place. When customers were browsing without necessarily having specific intent to purchase, a healthy default led to lower sales of the product than an unhealthy default. The weighted means of net default effect and net dodge effect were 25.6% and 6.9%, respectively, suggesting that the magnitude of dodge effect is roughly 27% of the size of the default effect.
Defaults	Signing up for an organic food box scheme (self-nudging) is a way to drive sustainable (pro-environmental) consumption behavior in the long run.

Authors, Year, Journal, Country	Participants
Benito-Ostolaza, J. M. et al. 2021 Social Science & Medicine Spain	N = 247 45% of the participants were girls and 55% were boys, students of 7 schools. The students were randomly assigned to the different treatments: 84 students participated in the control treatment, 83 in the positive treatment, and 80 in the negative treatment. Depending on the treatment group, the child was (i) not exposed to special visual stimuli (control), (ii) exposed to posters with a happy emoji surrounded by fruits (positive treatment), or (iii) exposed to posters with a sad emoji surrounded by highly processed and sugary foods (negative treatment). Subsequently, the child was directed to a table where the snacks were covered with a box that displayed the same visual stimulus as the poster (or no stimulus, for the control group).
Krpan, D. and Houtsma, N. 2020 Journal of Environmental Psychology United Kingdom	N = 11,066 (3 large pre-registered online studies)
Britwum, K. and Yiannaka, A. 2019 Journal of Behavioral and Experimental Economics United States	N = 1.842 (out of 2.999 demographically representative of the United States population)

Focus area	Key Findings
Framing	Positive visual stimuli increased the probability of healthy snack choice among girls by 26%. Negative visual stimuli do not seem to affect snack choice. The probability of choosing a healthy snack is significantly affected by the previous day snack choice. Those boys whose previous-day snack was fruit have a higher probability of choosing the healthy snack than those whose previous day snack contained a sandwich, highly processed or sugary food. The opposite effect was found in girls.
Framing	A pro-environmental frame (i.e., "Environmentally Friendly Main Courses for a Happy Planet"), a social frame (i.e., "Refreshing Main Courses for Relaxing Conversations"), and a neutral frame (i.e., vegetarian and non-vegetarian dishes mixed in the same section "Main Courses") all increased the likelihood of vegetarian choice compared to a vegetarian frame (i.e., "Vegetarian Main Courses"). Percentage of participants who made a vegetarian choice under different conditions: Study 1: Pro-environmental frame 22.1%, Social frame 18.7%, Vegetarian frame 12.8%. Study 2: Pro-environmental frame 25.8%, Social frame 22%, Neutral menu 21.6%, Vegetarian frame 16.1%. Study 3: Pro-environmental frame 24.5%, Neutral menu 24.3%, Vegetarian frame 18%.
Framing	Both loss-framed and gain-framed messages convincingly influenced safety perceptions of food under low issue involvement. Under high issue involvement, however, only the loss-framed message influenced consumers' safety perceptions. The two variables in the health risk perceptions segment, Risk from E. coli and Risk from technologies, were significant at better than the 1% level in the two regressions. Participants who believed they were more at risk from E. coli bacteria showed greater concern and were more likely to report greater perceived likelihood of an E. coli infection when consuming hamburgers. Likewise, participants who were apprehensive about the risks of meat products that had undergone different food production interventions such as irradiation, hormone use in livestock, or animal cloning (risk from technologies) were approximately 6% more likely to be concerned, with a similarly high perceived likelihood (5%) of an E. coli infection from hamburger consumption.

Authors, Year, Journal, Country	Participants
Cerezo-Prieto, M. and Frutos-Esteban, F. J. 2021 Atención Primaria Spain	N = 1122 Menus by university students. The questionnaire was answered by 48 university students who participated in the experiment. The menus were labeled with nutritional information. Next, posters with nutritional information were made with a color scale corresponding to traffic light for each dish (green, yellow, or red).
Hoenink, J. C. et al. 2021 International Journal of Behavioral Nutrition and Physical Activity Netherlands	On-shelf sugar labels were implemented by 30 Dutch supermarkets. Non-alcoholic beverages were classified using a traffic-light labeling system and included the beverage categories "green" for sugar free ($< 1.25\,g/250\,ml$), "blue" for low sugar ($1.25-6.24\,g/250\,ml$), "yellow" for medium sugar ($6.25-13.5\,g/250\,ml$), and "amber" for high sugar ($> 13.5\,g/250\,ml$). Store-level data on beverage sales and revenue from 41 randomly selected supermarkets for 13 weeks pre-implementation and 21 weeks post-implementation were used for analysis. 11 stores that had not implemented the labels were used as comparisons.
Magdaleno, M. et al. 2021 Journal of American College Health United States	N = 111 (College students) The study evaluated the process of implementation and impact of a front-of-pack labeling intervention on purchases of labeled food products in a university market setting.
Mecheva, M. V. et al. 2021 Journal of Health Economics Indonesia	18 public primary schools in Central Jakarta

Focus area	Key Findings
Labeling	The experiment showed an improvement in the diet with the inclusion of information appealing to the healthiest choice, increasing the consumption of fruit, vegetables, legumes, yoghurt, fish, and white meat. There were statistically significant differences in all dishes: starter (χ^2 [4, n = 1,101] = 12.3, p <0.05), first course (χ^2 [6, n = 1,101] = 125, p <0.000), second course (χ^2 [6, n = 1,101] = 69.5, p <0.000) and dessert (χ^2 [4, n = 1,101] = 26.7, p <0.000). The students surveyed showed a high degree of receptivity to these health promotion tools. When asked about the influence of interventions on food choices, 32.4% acknowledged that they helped them to eat less French fries, 14.7% to eat more fruit, and 13.7% to eat more legumes. 12.8% to eat less pasta, 12.8% to eat more fish, 5.9% to eat more salad, and 2.9% to eat less meat.
Labeling	The changes in sales of beverages labelled green (B 3.4, 95% CI − 0.3; 7.0), blue (B 0.0, 95% CI − 0.6; 0.7), yellow (B 1.3, 95% CI − 0.9; 3.5), and amber (B 0.9, 95% CI − 5.5; 7.3) labels were not significantly different between intervention and comparison stores.
Labeling	Customer surveys revealed that only 42% noticed the front-of-pack sticker, and the majority (89%) did not purchase an item with the sticker.
Labeling Children were exposed to emoji labels encouraging healthy snacks, while others observed healthy or unhealthy snacking by peers. Additionally, cross-randomized groups of children watched a video on nutrition to study the interaction of information provision and nudging.	Overall, 69% of the children opted for the healthy snack. During nudge condition without the video, the healthy choice went up by a modest 4% over the control condition. The effect associated with the Negative peer treatment was very large. Among subjects who saw their peers with a chocolate cake, a mere 35% opted for the healthy snack, which translates to a 28%, or 44% reduction compared to the control condition. During nudge condition with the video, the Positive peer effect treatment was also modest (at about 4%), while the effect associated with the Negative peer treatment was again greater (a 36% or a 43% decrease).

Authors, Year, Journal, Country	Participants
Colson, G. and Grebitus, C. 2017 Agribusiness United States	N = 733 (Parents)
Policastro, P. et al. 2017 Obesity United States	N = 2,393 (Unique students purchased 6,730 meals)
Rising, J. C. and Bol, N. 2017 Health Communication United States	N = 179 University students (M = 20.15, SD = 1.42)
Santos, O. et al. 2020 Appetite Portugal	N = 475 (out of 746) (Portuguese adult population, aged 18–64 years)
Montagni, I. et al. 2020 Journal of Occupational and Environmental Medicine France, United States	Employees' purchase of food items in of an international company's cafeterias was monitored in 6 intervention sites (one in France and five in the United States) where healthy food items had green labels.
Szakaly, Z. et al. 2020 Foods Hungary	N = 32

Focus area	Key Findings
Labeling	Parents preferred—and were more likely to purchase—yogurts with a label denoting the food is a healthy choice for children. Crucially, parents with children who are overweight or obese, were most affected by the labels.
Labeling 3 message-based nudge interventions were used during the 7-week study. Calorie savings (self-interest), charity (prosocial), or charity-plus-calorie message posters were displayed in a college-based food franchise.	Calorie messaging was more effective than charity appeals at boosting water substitutions. Adding the charity appeal to the calorie messaging neither helped nor hurt the calorie messaging's impact. The effect of the combination poster was moderated by both the linear ($\beta = 0.0099$, 95% CI: 0.0018 to 0.0179) and quadratic ($\beta = -0.0006$, 95% CI: -0.0002 to -0.0011) effect of frequency of patronizing the restaurant.
Labeling	The odds of choosing a lower calorie salad option versus a higher calorie salad option were 2.69 times higher when calorie labels were displayed on a menu than when calorie labels were not displayed (OR = 2.69; 95% CI 1.40–5.16), which was significant ($p = 0.003$). Participants were more likely to choose a lower calorie beverage option when calorie labels were displayed on a menu than when calorie labels were not displayed (OR = 2.47; 95% CI 1.29–4.71), which was significant ($p = 0.006$). Calorie awareness was also significantly predictive of beverage choice ($p = 0.023$). Being aware of calories increased the odds of choosing a lower calorie beverage option (OR = 3.77; 95% CI 1.20–11.78).
Labeling	Traffic light labels received more favorable responses among the consumers when selecting food products, when the labels reflected the perceived nutritional quality (adjusted Odd Ratio (aOR) = 5.37, Confidence Interval (CI) 95% [3.87–7.44]) than the Guideline Daily Amounts (aOR = 5.37, CI 95% [3.67–7.01]), Nutri-Score (aOR = 4.72, CI 95% [3.42–6.52]) or the Health Star Rating (aOR = 3.28, CI 95% [2.40–4.48]).
Labeling	Workplace food labeling while using positive nudge can contribute to healthy eating habits among employees in worksite cafeterias. One year after the intervention, purchase of labeled items was higher in the French intervention site compared with the control ($p < 0.001$). This consumption was increasing 2 years after the intervention ($p < 0.001$). The percentage (+8.0% from T0 to T1) of sales of labeled items from the US sites confirmed the transferability of this intervention.
Labeling	In spite of all the food samples (cheeses) being identical, the healthy samples were associated with considerably less sensory pleasure. The results of the Wilcoxon test indicate that only the reduced fat label resulted in significantly lower willingness to purchase ($Z = -2.352$; $p = 0.019$) and the salt intensity of the product with the conventional label was rated lower ($Z = -2.231$; $p = 0.026$). The health-halo effect could be observed, resulting in

Authors, Year, Journal, Country	Participants
Szakaly, Z. et al. *(continue)*	
Seward, M. W. and Soled, D. R. 2020 Journal of American College Health United States	Intervention at Harvard University cafeterias
Benson, T. et al. 2019 Nutrients Ireland	N = 1039 (Adults, ages 18–64)
Manippa, V. et al. 2020 Appetite Italy	N = 62 Italian young-adults (M age 22.5, SD = 8) have been recruited by telephone. 30 males, 32 females of normal weight (M Body Mass Index = 23.1, SD = 3.6)
Dallas, S. K., Liu, P. J., and Ubel, P. A. 2019 Journal of Consumer Psychology United States	N = 157, 54.8% female, M Age = 21.38, SDAge = 5.00) at a chain restaurant on a college campus
Mazza, M. C. et al. 2018 Health Promotion Practice United States	A 21-month field study in a hospital cafeteria

Focus area	Key Findings
	the health promoting variants being automatically associated with worse palatability thus no significant changes could be detected, either in liking or in willingness to purchase even after the tasting.
Labeling	Food labeling may lead to unintended consequences and exacerbate eating disorders. Women with anorexia nervosa or bulimia nervosa ordered significantly fewer calories, and women with binge-eating disorder ordered significantly more calories when using calorie-labeled menus. When asked whether traffic-light labels increased the risk of developing eating disorders, 16% of participants said they did and 47% said traffic-light labels might exacerbate existing eating disorders.
Labeling	Nutrition and Health Claims (NHCs) have been found to influence perceptions of food and consumption behavior. Perceptions and the characteristics of products displaying claims impacted believability, as well as purchasing behavior and consumption. Respondents were more likely to believe the NHCs (57%) and were slightly health conscious with a mean GHI score of 4.3 (maximum possible 7). Respondents believed they had relatively good knowledge of NHCs with a mean score of 10.23 (range 3 to 15). However, actual (objective) NHC knowledge was relatively low with a mean score of 2.32 from a maximum of 5. Individuals were motivated to process NHCs, with a mean motivation score of 9.86 (minimum possible 3, maximum possible 15). With regards to the recall of claims that were used in the survey, participants had a median score of 4 out of a possible 6 (minimum 0 and maximum 6), indicating general awareness of the NHCs used in the survey.
Labeling	The visual perception of a product and the ability to categorize it play a central role in food choice. Foods were categorized as healthier when, on the visual analogical scale the "Healthy" label was on the left and the "Unhealthy" on the right. Also, when presented on the left side, low-calorie was preferred compared to high-calorie food. The frequency distribution in the use of healthiness-related labels and calories-related labels differed significantly from a chance distribution ($\chi^2 (1) = 105.42$, $p < 0.001$) with a prevalent use of healthiness-related labels (57.7%) compared to calories-related ones (42.3%).
Labeling	The diners were randomly assigned to one of three conditions: left calories (n = 46), right calories (n = 58), or no calories (n = 53). Providing calorie counts on restaurants' menus to the left of food items decreased calories ordered by 16.31%. This effect was reversed e.g., among Hebrew speakers, who read from right to left.
Labeling	The addition of caloric information to traffic light labeling had a positive effect on the purchase of healthy chips in a hospital cafeteria (a 5.4 percentage increase (p = 0.001)). Some interventions, however, triggered compensatory behavior resulting in the

Authors, Year, Journal, Country	Participants
Mazza, M. C. et al. *(continue)*	
Benson, T. et al. 2018 Nutrients Ireland	N = 78
Castellari, E. et al. 2018 Bio-Based and Applied Economics Italy	N = 930 (about 84% were students) Experiment in a university cafeteria
Fisher, G. 2018 Appetite United States	N = 87 (Students; 71% female; mean age = 21.2)
Slapø, H. B. and Karevold, K. I. 2019 Frontiers in Sustainable Food Systems Norway	University cafeteria in Oslo
Reinoso-Carvalho, F. et al. 2021 Frontiers in Psychology N/A The participants were recruited on Prolific Academic	N = 496 (62.50% males, Mean of age 25.71 years, SD = 7.91). 8 different versions of packaging were produced for this experiment. They included two variations of packaging type (jar vs. bag), two variations of packaging transparency (transparent vs. opaque), and two variations of labeling (labeled vs. unlabeled). The following hypothesis were tested:

Focus area	Key Findings
	purchase of unhealthy items. Traffic light labeling was associated with a 2.9 percentage increase in healthy beverage sales ($p < 0.0001$). The subsequent phases incorporated the control conditions, eliminating the beneficial effect of traffic light labeling. For instance, color grouping (Phase 14) reduced healthy beverage purchases by 2% ($p < 0.0001$), social norms (Phase 10) decreased healthy purchases by 1.7% ($p < 0.01$), Oppositional pairing (Phase 12) decreased healthy purchases by 6.9% ($p = 0.01$).
Labeling	Nutrition and health claims ("Low in fat", "With plant sterols", "Fuller for longer") influenced fillingness perceptions of foods (cereal, soup, lasagna, and yoghurt). Yet, there was little influence the claims had on the perception of tastiness, healthiness, or the selected portion size. Knowledge was found to be a key influence on how claims are perceived.
Labeling	The provision of nutritional information by itself can have zero or low impact unless it synergizes with other instruments such as nutritional education, social norms, and nudges. Results showed students tended to be more reluctant to change their food selections (coefficients were negative and significant).
Labeling	Nutrition labeling reduced valuations of food through multiple health and taste channels. The presence of health information changed the importance individuals place on tastiness. However, there was no evidence for an attribute perception mechanism in the taste domain (no label: M = 0.70, SD = 0.53; nutrition: M = 0.55, SD = 0.59; $t(85) = 1.21$, $p = 0.232$).
Labeling	Three different labeling systems were tested on warm dishes (traffic-light labels with three symbols: red, yellow, and green; a single-green label that only labeled the environmentally friendliest dishes, and a single-red label that only labeled the least environmentally friendly option. Posters were placed in the cafeteria, explaining the labeling systems and the climate impact of different food categories. The study showed that traffic-light labels in combination with posters could improve the eco-friendliness of food choices in a cafeteria setting, at least short-term. The traffic-light labels reduced sales of meat dishes with 9% in the period 1 ($p < 0.1$) but not in period 2. Sales share of fish or vegetarian dishes were not impacted. Single-green and single-red labeling had no effect on sales share of fish or vegetarian dishes.
Labeling/Packing	The results suggest that the presence (vs. absence) of labeling triggered the highest ratings on most assessed attributes (product quality, healthiness, lightness, sweetness, crumbliness, price, tastiness, greediness for product, product/packaging appeal). Moreover, transparent (vs. opaque) packaging tends to yield higher expectations concerning this product's quality (i.e., product liking, package liking, greediness), though it has an opposite effect on the expected healthiness of such cookies.

Authors, Year, Journal, Country	Participants
Reinoso-Carvalho, F. et al. *(continue)*	H1: Changes in the visual appearance of packaging, in terms of presence (vs. absence) of label, packaging type (jar vs. bag), and transparency (vs. opaqueness) will modulate the expectations for dietary cookies in digital environments. H1a: The presence vs. absence of labeling will principally modulate aspects related to the expected healthiness of this product (calories, healthiness, lightness). H1b: A jar will most likely trigger sweeter and/or smoother sensations for the cookies, when compared to a bag type of packaging. H1c: A transparent packaging will create higher expectations concerning specific sensory (e.g., sweetness, crumbliness) and qualitative (e.g., greediness, preference, price) aspects of cookies flavor.
Zeballos, E., Mancino, L., and Lin, B. H. 2020 Food Policy United States	N = 4,826 The data come from the USDA's National Household Food Acquisition and Purchase Survey (FoodAPS). In total, there were 52,612 food events with a total of 259,124 items acquired or purchased. 98.9% of these events, had nutrition information and quantities.
Dolgopolova, I. et al. 2021 Sustainability Germany	N = 994 Young adults were nudged to reduce calories in a fast-food order.
Nagatomo, W., Saito, J., and Kondo, N. 2019 International Journal of Behavioral Nutrition and Physical Activity Japan	N^{i} = 7537 N^{ii} = 7826 In this crossover trial at 26 local restaurants, a 1-week campaign offered a 50-yen cash-back payment to customers ordering vegetable-rich meals.
Huang, J. et al. 2021 Journal of Sensory Studies China	N = 112 Adults (mean age = 21.8 ± 2.1 years; 41 males and 71 females) The participants first completed the Self-Construal Scale and then used a mouse to click on all the pronouns while reading an essay shown on the

Focus area	Key Findings
	The multivariate tests showed a main effect of packaging labeling and transparency ($p \leq 0.001$ for both), as well as an interaction effect of packaging labeling-transparency ($p \leq 0.001$), packaging type-transparency ($p \leq 0.001$), and with all of the three packaging factors combined ($p = 0.035$). No interaction effects with age ($p = 0.250$) or gender ($p = 0.210$) were found.
Monetary nudges	Shoppers using cash purchased a larger proportion of healthy items. This nudging effect was primarily driven by food-away-from-home purchases. Using cash increased the share of healthy items purchased for away-from-home consumption relative to non-healthy items by 3% when weighting each item by its share of total cost and total grams and by 2% when weighting each item by its percentage of total calories.
Multicomponent nudges (a combination of an order assistant and color-coded system)	The effect of nudges was slightly increasing at higher BMI levels. In the combined treatment, hunger and negative affect significantly moderated the effect of nudges. Participants in the order assistant (OA) treatment ordered 208 kcal less than in the no treatment condition ($F = 26.84$, $p < 0.01$). Participants who faced the color-coded system (CCS) treatment ordered 225 kcal less than in the no treatment condition ($F = 31.96$, $p < 0.01$). In the combined OA&CCS treatment, participants ordered 250 kcal less than in the no treatment condition ($F = 38.29$, $p < 0.01$).
Monetary nudges	Cash-back payment to customers ordering vegetable-rich meals raised healthy food choices. 511 respondents out of 7537 customers (6.8%) and 704 respondents out of 7826 customers (9.0%), ordered vegetable-rich meals. The covariate-adjusted proportion of vegetable-rich meal orders was 1.50 times higher (95% confidence interval [CI]: 1.29 to 1.75), which increased daily sales by 1.77 times (95% CI: 1.11 to 2.83).
	The priming × plate size × plate color ANOVA revealed a significant main effect of plate size, $F(1, 110) = 86.68$, $p < 0.001$, $\eta p^2 = 0.44$. The participants were willing to pay significantly more for the same noodles when they were presented on a small plate ($M = ¥ 9.0$) than when presented on a large plate ($M = ¥ 7.0$). The results also revealed a significant interaction term between

Authors, Year, Journal, Country	Participants
Huang, J. et al. *(continue)*	computer screen (i.e., the self-construal priming). Next, the participants were asked to complete the image rating task, and the six photos of Asian noodles were shown in a random order, one at a time. When viewing each photo, they were instructed to indicate their willingness-to-pay (WTP) for the noodles shown on the photo by specifying the amount of money (in CNY) they were willing to pay for the food. They were also asked to rate how pleasant and how familiar the noodles looked, as well as how congruent the noodles were with the plates, all on seven-point scales with higher values indicating the increased intensity of the attribute rated. They were also asked to rate their expectations concerning the sweetness and saltiness of the noodles on seven-point scales. At the end of the study, the participants were asked to indicate how frequently they eat Asian noodles in daily life by choosing one option from "never," "occasionally," "sometimes," and "often."
Trakman, G. et al. 2021 International Journal of Environmental Research and Public Health Australia	N^i = 88 N^{ii} = 76 N^{iii} = 22 (Basketball managers)

Focus area	Key Findings
Multicomponent nudges (Priming, Size) 2 (priming: interdependent or independent self-construal priming) × 2 (plate size: large or small) × 3 (plate color: red, blue, or white) mixed design was used. Specifically, priming was treated as a between-participants factor, whereas plate color and plate size were both treated as within-participants factors.	priming and plate size, $F (1, 220) = 4.09$, $p = 0.046$, $\eta p2 = 0.04$; whereas none of the other main or interaction effects was significant, all $Fs < 2.71$, $ps > 0.06$. The priming × plate size × plate color ANOVA revealed a significant main effect of plate size, $F (1, 110) = 73.50$, $p < 0.001$, $\eta p2 = 0.40$. The same noodles were rated as being more pleasant when they were presented on a small plate than on a large plate (3.8 vs. 3.2). The results also revealed a significant main effect of plate color, $F (2, 220) = 3.87$, $p = 0.022$, $\eta p2 = 0.03$. The priming × plate size × plate color ANOVAs revealed a significant main effect of plate size on the familiarity scores, $F (1, 110) = 50.21$, $p < 0.001$, $\eta p2 = 0.31$, and on the congruency scores, $F (1, 110) = 130.81$, $p < 0.001$, $\eta p2 = 0.54$. The same noodles served on a small plate looked more familiar and more congruent with this plate, compared to a large plate. The results also revealed a significant main effect of plate color on the familiarity ratings, $F (2, 220) = 14.42$, $p < 0.001$, $\eta p2 = .12$, and on the congruency ratings, $F (2, 220) = 18.35$, $p < 0.001$, $\eta p2 = 0.14$. The same noodles looked more familiar to the participants when they were shown on a white plate ($M = 4.5$) than on a red ($M = 4.0$) or a blue plate ($M = 4.0$), both $ts > 4.51$, $ps < 0.001$, Cohen's $ds > 0.40$; and these foods were also considered to be more congruent with a white plate ($M = 4.2$) than with a red ($M = 3.3$) or blue plate ($M = 3.6$), both $ts > 3.94$, $ps < 0.001$, Cohen's $ds > 0.47$. The difference between the red and blue plates was not significant on either measure, both $ts < 2.05$, $ps > 0.12$. None of other main or interaction effects were significant on either measure, all $Fs < 1.94$, $ps > 0.16$. The priming × plate size × plate color ANOVAs on these data revealed a significant main effect of plate size on the expected sweetness, $F (1, 110) = 5.58$, $p = 0.02$, $\eta p2 = 0.05$, and on the expected saltiness, $F (1, 110) = 5.18$, $p = 0.03$, $\eta p2 = 0.05$. The same noodles were expected to be sweeter and saltier when they were shown on a small plate than on a large plate.
Multi-component nudges (Labeling, positioning) A healthy canteen display, based on traffic light labeling (TLL) was set up at an Australian Basketball Association Managers' Convention and Trade Show. Basketball managers were surveyed on their perceptions of the display before (Survey 1) and after (Survey 2) visiting the display. Three months later they weresurveyed (Survey 3)on changes made to their community sport canteens.	Participants in Survey 1 believed stocking healthy foods and beverages was important (mean 8.5/10). Most respondents (92%) thought seeing a display of a healthy canteen would be useful. While just over a half of the respondents (52%) had heard of TLL, 91% rated their confidence in being able to classify foods based on the TLL as 5 or above (out of 10), with a mean confidence rating of 7.4. Nearly a half (45%) of the respondents thought having more healthy foods would have no impact on sales. Viewing the display (Survey 2) did not lead to a statistically significant change in mean rating for importance of stocking healthy options, t (-0.825), df = 162, p = 0.410. Likewise, there was no statistically significant change in confidence in classifying foods according to TLL between Survey 1 and Survey 2, t(-0.558), df = 162, p = 0.578. Mean rating for usefulness of the healthy-canteen display was 8.0 out of 10. 92% of respondents reported the healthy-canteen display had provided them with new ideas about

Authors, Year, Journal, Country	Participants
Trakman, G. et al. *(continue)*	
Ojwang, S. O. et al. 2021 Current Developments in Nutrition Kenya	N = 431 preschooler-caregiver pairs from 15 village-level clusters The sample was randomized into one control (three villages) and three treatment groups (four villages each). Treatments involved nutrition education through learning materials (preschooler treatment); through mobile phones (caregiver treatment); and to both preschoolers and their caregivers simultaneously (integrated treatment).
Just, D. R. et al. 2021 The European Journal of Development Research Nigeria	20 elementary schools The main hypotheses included: H1: Engaging school children in a song that stresses how orange-fleshed sweet potato (OFSP) can promote health, strength, power, and success will increase the average consumption of OFSP. H2: Displaying posters promoting OFSP using a known aspirational figure (in this case the soccer player John Obi Mekel) will increase the average consumption of OFSP. H3: Displaying posters that use age-appropriate communication to stress that OFSP can promote strength, power, and success will increase the average consumption of OFSP.
Stuber, J. M. et al. 2021 The American Journal of Clinical Nutrition Netherlands	N = 318 The participants completed a web-based virtual supermarket experiment. The aim was to investigate the single and combined effects of nudging (e.g., making healthy products salient), taxes (25% price increase), and/or subsidies (25% price decrease) across food groups (fruit and vegetables, grains, dairy, protein products, fats, beverages, snacks, and other foods).

Focus area	Key Findings
	foods to stock at their canteen and 75% reported they were inspired to make changes to their canteens. 50% were surprised by the differences between their perceptions of the healthfulness of foods and the traffic light labeling (TLL) ratings. 41% of respondents in Survey 3 (n = 9) had made changes to their community sport canteen as a result of visiting the display and 70% (n = 14) reported having plans to make changes.
Multi-component nudges (Priming, Framing, Social Norms)	The results of a zero-inflated Poisson regression showed that the phone-mediated and multichanneled nutrition education approaches significantly increased the number of days of orange-fleshed sweet potato (OFSP) consumption. The integrated nutrition education approach significantly increased the preschoolers' likelihood to consume OFSP, number of OFSP consumption days, and likelihood to consume it more than once per week by 11%, 77%, and 20%, respectively.
Multi-component nudges (Priming, Framing, Social Norms)	The behavioral interventions that engaged the students in a song or used aspirational figures (in this case, a professional soccer player) were effective in encouraging additional OFSP consumption, with orders increasing by 47g or more.
Multi-component nudges (Priming, salience)	Compared with the control condition, the combination of subsidies on healthy products and taxes on unhealthy products in the nudging and price salience condition was overall the most effective, as the number of healthy purchases from fruit and vegetables increased by 9% [incidence rate ratio (IRR) = 1.09; 95% CI: 1.02, 1.18], grains by 16% (IRR = 1.16; 95% CI: 1.05, 1.28), and dairy by 58% (IRR = 1.58; 95% CI: 1.31, 1.89), whereas the protein and beverage purchases did not significantly change. Regarding unhealthy purchases, grains decreased by 39% (IRR = 0.72; 95% CI: 0.63, 0.82) and dairy by 30% (IRR = 0.77; 95% CI: 0.68, 0.87), whereas beverage and snack purchases did not significantly change.

Authors, Year, Journal, Country	Participants
Loeb, K. L. et al. 2017 Appetite United States	N = 62 parents + 62 children
Friis, R. et al. 2017 PLOS ONE Denmark	N = 88
Kraak, V. et al. 2017 International Journal of Environmental Research and Public Health United States	N = 84 (restaurants)
Broers, V. J. V. et al. 2019 Appetite Belgium	2 studies conducted in sandwich restaurants in a university campus

Focus area	Key Findings
Multi-component nudges 2 randomized experiments (a children's breakfast selection study and a children's activity choice study) tested the effects of defaults and priming on parents' or other primary caregivers' health-related choices on behalf of their children.	Default condition, but not priming condition or the interaction between default and priming, significantly predicted menu choice (healthier vs. less healthy option). For the breakfast study, passive, or active parental selection of the optimal menu array for the child yielded consumption of healthier breakfast items. All children ate at least some of the food presented to them, similar to quantities consumed in the suboptimal breakfast array. In addition, there were no differences in consumption between those who were randomized to the optimal menu (i.e., who never saw the suboptimal choices) and those who switched from the suboptimal to the optimal breakfast.
Multi-component nudges (Priming, default, and perceived variety). The priming consisted of creating a leafy environment with green plants and an odor of herbs. In the default branch of the experiment, the salad was pre-portioned into a bowl containing 200g of vegetables. The third experiment divided the pre-mixed salad into each of its components, to increase the visual variety of vegetables, yet not providing an actual increase in items.	The default experiment successfully increased the energy intake from vegetables among the study participants (124 kcal vs. 90 kcal in control, $p < 0.01$). Both the priming condition and perceived variety reduced the total energy intake among the study participants (169 kcal, $p < 0.01$ and 124 kcal, $p < 0.01$, respectively), mainly through a decrease in the meat-based meal component.
Multi-component nudges A marketing-mix and choice-architecture framework was used to examine 8 strategies (i.e., place, profile, portion, pricing, promotion, healthy default picks, priming or prompting and proximity) to evaluate progress (i.e., no, limited, some or extensive) during the 10-year review period.	The study found that the US restaurant sector made limited progress to use pricing, profile (reformulation), priming (healthy defaults), promotion (responsible marketing) and prompting (labeling), and some progress to reduce portions to encourage healthy choices for American consumers during the 10-year period reviewed (2006 to early 2017). No evidence was available to assess progress for place (ambience and atmospherics) and proximity (positioning).
Multi-component nudges	The default-name nudge ("suggestion of the chef") increased the proportion of customers that choose the salsify soup during intervention days compared to non-intervention days, $p < 0.001$, OR: 1.70. The tasting nudge also increased the proportion of customers that choose the salsify soup from baseline to intervention, $p < 0.001$, OR: 6.17 and from baseline to post-intervention, $p < 0.01$, OR: 1.87, and decreased from intervention to post-intervention, $p < 0.001$, OR: 0.30.

Authors, Year, Journal, Country	Participants
Fitzgerald, S., Geaney, F., and Perry, I. J. 2019 Journal of Epidemiology and Community Health Ireland	N = 541 manufacturing employees (18–64 years)
Hamdi, N. et al. 2020 International Journal of Environmental Research and Public Health (IJERPH) United States	N = 1255 (Children in three rural elementary school cafeterias)
Ohlhausen, P. and Langen, N. 2020 Foods Germany	N^i = 100 N^{ii} = 420 N^{iii} = 820 (Three consecutive studies: two were conducted in university canteens and one in a business canteen.)
Cadario, R. and Chandon, P. 2020 Marketing Science United States, France	Analysis of 299 effect sizes derived from 90 articles and 96 field experiments
Knowles, D., Brown, K., and Aldrovandi, S. 2020 Appetite United Kingdom	N^i = 85 N^{ii} = 80 20 chocolate brownies that were either wrapped or unwrapped (Study 1, N = 85), or 250g of M&M's, either colorful or plain brown (Study 2, N = 80), were presented as effort and salience manipulations, respectively, to participants at either 20 cm or 70 cm distance. Consumption was measured as likelihood of consumption' (Yes/No) and 'actual consumption' (units/grams).

Focus area	Key Findings
Multi-component nudges	Combining nutrition education and smartphone nutrition intervention supported healthier food choices and better health status in term of QALYs. There were significant positive changes in intakes of saturated fat ($p = 0.013$), salt ($p = 0.010$) and nutrition knowledge ($p = 0.034$) between baselines and follow-up in the combined intervention versus the control. Significant changes in BMI (-1.2 kg/m2 ($p = 0.047$) were also observed in the combined intervention. System-level modification yielded the highest additional QALYs (€101.37/QALY) and annual net benefit for employers (€56.56/employee).
Multi-component nudges	An intervention consisting of decorations, creative names, social norming taste tests, and flavor station components in school cafeterias improved vegetable selection and fruit consumption. Fruit consumption increased at School 1 ($p < 0.05$) during the taste test and flavor station intervention months and School 2 ($p < 0.001$) during the creative names' intervention months compared to baseline. Odds of selecting a vegetable at School 3 were three times higher than baseline during the taste test intervention months (odds ratio (OR), 3.0; 95% confidence interval (CI), 1.3–6.5).
Multi-component nudges	Target dishes with descriptive name labels (DNLs) were most favored. Study participants preferred the descriptions 'regional' (about 15% choice increase) and 'sustainable' (about 20% choice increase). However, the combination of descriptive name labels (DNLs) and the decoy effect (by adding a less attractive decoy dish to a more attractive target dish) is not recommended for fostering sustainable food choices.
Multi-component nudges	Interventions are more effective at reducing unhealthy eating than increasing healthy eating or reducing total eating. The analysis shows that the average effect size of healthy eating nudges is $d = .23$, 95% CI [.16; .31]. Effect sizes increase as the focus of the nudges shifts from cognition ($d = 0.12$, -64 kcal) to affect ($d = 0.24$, -129 kcal) to behavior ($d = 0.39$, -209 kcal). Compared with the typical nudge study (measured by Cohen's standardized mean difference $d = 0.12$), one implementing the best nudge scenario can expect a sixfold increase in effectiveness ($d = 0.74$).
Multi-component nudges	Likelihood of consumption was positively predicted by perceived visual salience in both studies, and by distance in Study 2. Significant main effects of distance, $p < 0.001$, $\eta2 = 0.102$ (20 cm > 70 cm), effort, $p < 0.001$, $\eta2 = 0.089$ (unwrapped > wrapped), and distance × effort interaction, $p = 0.003$, $\eta2 = 0.111$, were observed in Study 1 for actual consumption. A main effect of distance was found in Study 2 for actual consumption, $p < 0.001$, $\eta2 = 0.062$ (20 cm > 70 cm). No main effect of distance, $p = 0.12$, or color type, $p = 0.53$, or interaction between distance and color type, $p = 0.064$, was found.

Authors, Year, Journal, Country	Participants
Dos Santos, Q. et al. 2020 European Journal of Nutrition Denmark, France, Italy, and United Kingdom	N = 360 (Aged 12–19) (A cross-sectional quasi-experimental study in restaurants in four European countries: Denmark, France, Italy, and United Kingdom)
Vermote, M. et al. 2020 Appetite Belgium	N = 33,836 (Menus with dessert) In an on-campus university restaurant, nudges were employed as follows: placement of (1) Food Triangle posters in the restaurant, (2) green heart icons above the fruit stands, and (3) substitution, and (4) social norm messages at the fruit stands. During baseline (no intervention) and four intervention weeks, dessert sales were registered and analyzed separately for both sexes, students, and staff categories (based on academic degree).
Chapman, L. E. et al. 2019 Public Health Nutrition United States	In two grocery stores in rural counties in central North Carolina, the 3 nudges were implemented: a ‚cognitive fatigue' experiment, in which floor arrows guided customers to the produce sections; a ‚scarcity' experiment, in which one sign in one area of the produce section portrayed a ‚limited amount' message; and a ‚product placement' experiment, where granola bars were moved into the candy bar aisle. 118 and 125 shoppers of the two stores completed customer surveys.
Reynolds, P. et al. 2019 Social Science and Medicine United Kingdom	N = 7058 (An online study assessed public acceptability of interventions as follows: availability, labeling, size, and tax to change a range of behaviors including the consumption of alcohol, tobacco, and food).
Mistura, M. et al. 2019 Nutrients Canada	N = 340 The efficacy of a 'feasible' nudge intervention to increase the purchase of vegetables in a university residence cafeteria was examined by first year university students (ages 17–19) in British Columbia.

Focus area	Key Findings
Multi-component nudges	The nudging strategy ("dish of the day") did not show a difference on the choice of the vegetable-based option among adolescents tested using the Pearson chi-square test. (p = 0.80 for Denmark and France and p = 0.69 and p = 0.53 for Italy and UK, respectively). Yet, food choice questionnaire, social norms and attitudes towards vegetable nudging were positively associated with the choice of the vegetable-based dish (this led to a 94%, 16%, and 5% higher likelihood in choosing the vegetable-based dish). Male adolescents were 57% less likely to choose the vegetable-based dish.
Multi-component nudges	The use of the Flemish Food Triangle and the green heart intervention materials (e.g., cognitive nudges and social norms) resulted in increase in fruit purchase. After seven weeks of follow-up, significant fruit sale increases were established for all subgroups compared to baseline. At 30 weeks follow-up, the effect for bachelor's degree staff disappeared. The majority of the respondents (66.4%) had noticed at least one of the nudges, while only 3.4% indicated to have adjusted their dessert choice as a result of the nudges.
Multi-component nudges	In convenience stores, there were no significant differences between sales of the promoted items during the intervention period for any of the nudges when implemented individually. However, compared with baseline sales, implementation of all three nudges simultaneously was associated with an increase in sales during the intervention period based on proportional computations (p = 0.001, ANOVA).
Multi-component nudges	Acceptability differed across policy, behavior, and evidence communication (all ps < 0.001). Labeling was the most acceptable policy (supported by 78% of the participants), then size, tax, and availability of alcohol, tobacco, and food (47%). Tobacco use was the most acceptable behavior to be targeted by policies (73%) compared with policies targeting alcohol (55%) and food (54%). Asserting effectiveness increased acceptability; quantifying it had no added impact.
Multi-component nudges	Fresh vegetables placed at the hot food table encouraged vegetable purchase. However, to be considered effective, the percentage of non-overlapping data (PND) must be >50%, and ideally >70%, and that did not occur in this study. The effect of placement, sensory and cognitive nudges was more apparent with female purchases (30% PND).

Authors, Year, Journal, Country	Participants
Samek, A. 2019 Journal of Economic Behavior and Organization United States	N = 1400 (Children)
Cheung, T. T. L. et al. 2019 BMC Public Health Netherlands	3 types of nudges were implemented at a take-away food vendor at a large academic hospital: 1) an accessibility nudge that placed fruits at the front counter; 2) a salience nudge that presented healthy bread rolls to be more visually attractive; 3) a social proof nudge that conveyed yoghurt as a popular choice.
Hoenink, J. C. et al. 2020 International Journal of Behavioral Nutrition and Physical Activity Netherlands	N = 346 (Dutch adults, low and high socio-economic position, median age: 32.5) A little over 49% of participants had a high level of educational and almost 33% had a high income. Participants were exposed to five within-subject study conditions (control, nudging, pricing, price salience and price salience with nudging) and randomized to one of 3 between-subject study arms (a 25% price increase on unhealthy products, a 25% discount on healthy products, or a 25% price increase and discount).
Flores, D. et al. 2019 Journal of Experimental Psychology-Applied United States	N = 134 (40% female, Mage = 31.3, MBMI = 25.8) Four experiments in a cafeteria (Indulgent dish first, healthy dish first, indulgent dish last and healthy dish last) uncovered. The interaction effect on food choices and overall caloric intake.

Focus area	Key Findings
Multi-component nudges	Choice architecture, pledge and material incentives increased choice of the healthier milk by 15%in schoolchildren. Giving the option to set a goal increased choice of the healthier milk by 10%.
Multi-component nudges	The accessibility nudge significantly increased the sales of fresh fruit. During the baseline week a total amount of 90 pieces of fruit were sold. The total amount of fruit sales increased to 156 during the nudge week, which is equivalent to a 73.3% increase. Furthermore, a total amount of 164 pieces of fruit were sold during the nudge and disclosure week. This was an 82.2% increase compared to the baseline week and a slight increase of 5.1% compared to the nudge week. The impact of the salience nudge was limited presumably due to existing preferences or habits that typically facilitate bread purchases. During the baseline week a total of 291 healthy bread rolls were sold. The total amount of healthy bread rolls increased to 318 during the nudge week, which is equivalent to a 9.3% increase. During the nudge and disclosure week a total of 327 healthy bread rolls were sold, which was a 12.4% increase compared to the baseline week and a 2.8% increase relative to the nudge week. As the sales of the yoghurt shakes was low, the impact of the social proof nudge remained unexamined.
Multi-component nudges	Combining salient pricing (price increases and discounts) and nudging strategies resulted in increases in the percentage of healthy products for people with both low and high socio-economic position. Nudging and non-salient pricing strategies alone did not statistically significantly increase healthy food purchases, whereas a combination of salient price increases and discounts led to an increase in the percentage of healthy food purchases ($B = 4.5$, 95% CI = 2.6; 6.4). Combining salient pricing and nudging strategies led to increases in the percentage of healthy products in all three pricing arms, with largest effects found in the combined price increase and discount arm ($B = 4.0$, 95%, CI = 2.0; 6.0).
Multi-component nudges	Proximity, indulgence, and cognitive nudges (i.e., order of food presentation) work together to influence food consumption. The interaction effect of dessert presentation order and dessert type on actual calories consumed was found, $F(1, 123) = 26.63$, $p < 0.001$, $\eta p2 = .18$. The participants consumed significantly fewer calories when the indulgent dessert was positioned first (M = 582, SE = 18.28) than when the healthy dessert was positioned first (M = 830, SE = 33.60), $t(63) = 6.64$, $p < 0.001$, d = 1.63. In contrast, there was no significant difference in the number of calories patrons had consumed when the indulgent dessert was positioned last (M = 743, SE = 39.28) versus when the healthy dessert was positioned last (M = 683, SE = 27.24), $t(60) = 1.28$, $p > 0.10$.

Authors, Year, Journal, Country	Participants
Flores, D. et al. *(continue)*	
Marcano-Olivier, M. et al. 2019 International Journal of Behavioral Nutrition and Physical Activity United Kingdom	N = 176 (Intervention n = 86, control n = 90) The intervention in four primary schools included improved positioning and serving of fruit, accompanied by attractive labelling of both fruit and vegetables on offer.
Winkler, G. et al. 2018 Ernahrungs Umschau Germany	A study was conducted in a university cafeteria (on average, 1,100 students and over 168 members of staff every day) and in a school cafeteria.

Focus area	Key Findings
	Experiment 1: A field study in a real-life cafeteria showed that when an indulgent (healthy) dish is the first item, lower-calorie (higher-calorie) dishes are subsequently chosen, and overall caloric consumption is lower (higher). Experiments 2 and 3 replicated these effects in the context of ordering food on a website. Experiment 4 further revealed that high (vs. low) cognitive load alters the identified interaction effect, such that when an indulgent dish is the first item, higher-calorie dishes are subsequently chosen.
Multi-component nudges	Significant increases were found in the intervention condition for consumption of fruit ($F (1, 86) = 17.21$, $p = 0.001$), vitamin C ($F (1, 86) = 11.39$, $p = 0.001$), and fiber ($F (1, 86) = 22.78$, $p = 0.001$), from baseline to follow-up. No significant changes in consumption were identified in the intervention condition for vegetables ($F (1, 86) = 0.52$, $p = 0.473$) and sugar ($F (1, 86) = 3.52$, $p = 0.064$), from baseline to follow-up.
Multi-component nudges	Availability, visibility, and accessibility of healthy meals in a university cafeteria marked changes in behavior in the desired direction among both students and staff. Yet school cafeteria results were less consistent. In the long term, the choice of healthy food and drink increased up to 10% were observed among both students and staff. Among students, the proportion of vegan or vegetarian mains increased continuously despite the comparatively high initial proportion of just over 50% at the beginning: by +6.4% in the short term ($p \leq 0.001$), by +9.4% in the medium-term ($p \leq 0.001$), and by +10.1% in the long-term ($p \leq 0.001$). The number of students who chose salad as a side dish increased by 2.1% ($p \leq 0.001$) in the short term, by 5.5% ($p \leq 0.001$) in the medium-term, and by 4.7% ($p \leq 0.001$) in the long-term compared to the baseline value. A desired effect was also found in terms of the selection of fresh fruit for dessert. The proportion of students who chose fruit increased by 2.7% ($p \leq 0.001$) in the short-term, by 2.4% ($p \leq 0.001$) in the medium-term, and by 2.0% ($p \leq 0.001$) in the long-term compared to the baseline value. In the case of wholegrain snacks, a short and medium-term effect of a 2.6% increase ($p \leq 0.001$) was observed, but in the long-term, the baseline level was reached. The proportion of sweets among student diners decreased by 0.8% in the short-term ($p = 0.24$), by 3.1% in the medium-term ($p \leq 0.001$) and by 2.9% in the long-term ($p \leq 0.001$), although the proportion of ice cream increased by 8.3% in the medium-term, i.e., in the early summer months ($p \leq 0.001$). The proportion of water in reference to all selected drinks increased in the short term by 11.7% ($p \leq 0.001$), in the medium-term by 9.2% ($p \leq 0.001$) and in the long-term by 8.2% ($p \leq 0.001$).

Authors, Year, Journal, Country	Participants
Velema, E. et al. 2018 American Journal of Clinical Nutrition Netherlands	14 simultaneously executed strategies based on nudging and social marketing theories, involving product, price, placement, and promotion in 30 worksite cafeterias throughout the 12-week intervention period.
Thorndike, A. N. 2020 Social Science and Medicine United States	The study deals with the functioning of healthy choice architecture in the supermarket.
Van Rookhuijzen, M. and De Vet, E. 2020 Public Health Nutrition Netherlands	Eight products were added to the range of foods and drinks in two football canteens for three and 15 weeks, serving as a baseline period. In the intervention period, these products were promoted with the use of salience, scarcity, availability, and default nudges, for 26 and 16 weeks, respectively. Questionnaires were filled outby 70 and 59 visitors of the canteens. Four interviews were held with board members and canteen personnel.
Kurz, V. 2018 Journal of Environmental Economics and Management Sweden	Field experiment with 2 restaurants to test if nudging can increase the consumption of vegetarian food.
Bevet, S. et al. 2018 PLoS ONE United States	N^i = 681 (pre-survey) N^{ii} = 128 2 interventions were implemented to assess the "late-night dining" options in a university dining hall. In the first, a "veggie-heavy" entrée was added at the beginning of the line.

Focus area	Key Findings
Multi-component nudges	The study showed significant positive effects on purchases for 3 of the 7 product groups: healthier sandwiches, cheese, and fruit. A significantly higher number of healthier sandwiches was sold in the intervention cafeterias than in the control cafeterias (i.e., mean ± SD: 3.3 ± 3.1 compared with 0.9 ± 2.2, respectively) per 100 customers. However, the purchases of regular sandwiches decreased (from 14.2 ± 7.8 to 11.3 ± 7.1) in the intervention cafeterias. In the control group, the sales of this product per 100 customers remained constant (from 13.0 ± 9.3 to 13.4 ± 9.1). For the cheese product group, a significant increase was observed in the purchasing of the low-fat cheese in the intervention group during the intervention phase compared with the control group (From 1.3 ± 1.7 to 4.8 ± 3.5 compared with 2.3 ± 4.3 to 3.3 ± 7.1, respectively). The consumers in the intervention group bought an additional 0.7 pieces of fruit per 100 consumers compared with the control group.
Multi-component nudges	Healthy choice architecture is more likely to be effective if default choices are compatible with shoppers' personal preferences or long-term goals. Combining product placement nudges with other salient interventions (price incentives or simplified health labels) are more effective.
Multi-component nudges	Nudges seem to be a valuable addition to other efforts to combat unhealthy eating. Mixed results were obtained regarding the suitability of nudges to be used to promote healthy eating in sports clubs. Sales and revenue data showed positive trends, the intervention was seen as acceptable by all stakeholders and the intervention had a large reach. However, adherence to the intervention in both canteens and the effects of the nudges on the total consumption pattern were low. Factors were identified that promoted or hindered the intervention at an individual, interventional, and organizational level.
Multi-component nudges	The salience of the healthy option was increased by changing the menu order and enhancing the visibility of the vegetarian dish. The nudges increased the share of vegetarian lunches sold by 6% on average. The change in behavior was partly persistent, as the share of vegetarian lunches sold remained 4% higher after the intervention ended than before the experiment. The intervention reduced food-related greenhouse gas (GHG) emissions from food sales by around 5%.
Multi-component nudges	College students who did not dine late at night placed a higher value on health than students attending late-night dining. Nudges appear to have been partially successful in increasing the choice of vegetable-heavy entrées and snack foods. An ANOVA test compared Student Health Scores between those that reported late-night dining at least weekly (mean Health Score = 3.75, SD = 1.88) and those who reported going less than weekly/never

Authors, Year, Journal, Country	Participants
Bevet, S. et al. *(continue)*	In the second, a snack-food bar was set up to cater to students who did not want to stand in the long entrée line and preferred a snack.
Raghoebar, S. et al 2019 Appetite Netherlands	N = 173 (From 17 to 65 years of age, M = 29.15, SD = 12.67, 76.9% were female. 59.5% of the participants were students.) Participants were shown photographs and asked the following open question: "Which elements in the photograph may encourage and/or discourage one to obtain foods?"
Bauer, M. J. et al. 2021 Appetite Germany	N = 5300 (Potential corporate cafeteria customers)

Focus area	Key Findings
	(mean Health Score = 4.23, SD = 1.94), which was statistically significant difference between the groups ($F = 9.68$, $p < 0.01$). Students that exclusively wanted less healthy options were significantly more likely to have a lower Health Score (M = 2.66, SD = 1.57) than other students (M = 4.72, SD = 1.77, $F = 124.28$, $p < 0.001$. There was no statistically significant difference between a student's Health Score and the foods they actually chose at late-night dining, ($F = 0.39$, $p = 0.883$), indicating that considering health when opting for late-night dining options did not relate to actual entrée choice. When vegetable-heavy entrée was added to the main entrée line for three weeks, researchers observed 2,397 trips through the entrée line, 28% by females and 72% by males.
Multi-component nudges	Physical cues (e.g., consumption traces, product availability) associated with either descriptive or injunctive social norm connotations physically embedded in food environments might guide food consumption. In the 40 photographs, 128 different specific physical cues were identified that could be related to social norms (e.g., 'middle shelf in refrigerator', 'fixed size of bowl', or 'plastic wrap on product plate') which in the end were categorized into 18 higher level conceptual categories (e.g., placement, unit size, or (un)covered presentation).
Multi-component nudges: Study 1: Different goal-related email messages associated with the green line (GL) just before lunchtime. Study 2: Limiting easy access to the GL alternative by reducing the number of "all inclusive" payment terminals. Study 3: Increasing salience of the GL by sticking guiding green footprints on the floor from cafeteria entrance to GL terminal.	Study 1: The effect was small but statistically significant (beta = -0.04, $p = 0.04$, 95% CI [-0.08, -001]). Testing the groups individually, it was observed that the negative effect was mainly driven by the group of interns, who showed a stronger and highly significant reduction in their healthy choices (beta = -0.09, $p < 0.001$, 95% CI [-0.14, -0.04]). Significant effects on trainees were not observed. Study 2: The results for the group of regular employees indicated a significant increase in the probability of choosing the Green Line (beta = 0.08, $p < 0.001$, 95% CI [0.05, 0.12]). No significant difference was observed for trainees and interns treated as one group (beta = 0.01, $p = 0.76$, 95% CI [-0.06, 0.09]), nor when analyzed separately. Customers identified as guests showed an increase in Green Line use, which was, however, not statistically significant (beta = 0.05, $p = 0.21$, 95% CI [-0.03, 0.13]). Study 3: Increasing salience through footprints intervention showed no effect on the group of regular employees (beta = -0.01, $p = 0.46$, 95% CI [-0.03, 0.01]), nor was there an effect on the pooled sample of trainees and interns (beta = -0.02, $p = 0.27$, 95% CI [-0.06, 0.16]). When the group of young employees was analyzed separately, trainees showed a small positive but insignificant effect on Green Line choice after the implementation of the footsteps (beta = 0.03, $p = 0.10$, 95% CI [-0.01, 0.08]).

Authors, Year, Journal, Country	Participants
Vandenbroele, J. et al. 2021 Organizational Behavior and Human Decision Processes Belgium	N^i = 100 000 Individual customers in 8 stores during a 2-month period. N^{ii} = 231 Undergraduate students (111 men; Mage = 20.55, SD = 1.06) The meat substitutes were placed in a more visible location and they were offered next to a similar meat-based product (i.e., pairwise presentation).
Mikkelsen, Bent E. et al. 2021 Food Quality and Preference Denmark	N = 7766 4 canteens for students (age 16–23) of vocational schools.
Wyse, R. et al. 2019 American Journal of Clinical Nutrition Australia	N = 1938 This study investigated whether an intervention to position fruit and vegetable snack items as the first and last menu items in an online school canteen ordering system increased the selection of those items. Students (1203 intervention, 735 control) placed at least one online lunch order and were included in the study, with 16,109 orders placed throughout the study.
Kim, J. et al. 2019 Cornell Hospitality Quarterly New Zealand	N^i = 202 US residents (average age = 32.7, SD = 7.4, 48.0% female) were asked to select one out of four different tacos in an imaginary Mexican restaurant and select one out of the four different wines. N^{ii} = 155 US residents (average age = 36.2, SD = 11.8, 49.0% female) were asked to imagine that they were drinking a cocktail in a bar and select one out of five different cocktails.
Van Gestel, L. C. et al. 2018 Psychology and Health Netherlands	N = 186 (Kiosk customers) The effect of a food repositioning nudge on healthy food choice was investigated in a kiosk for eight weeks.

Focus area	Key Findings
Positioning	Both product visibility and pairwise presentation increase sales of meat substitutes (a 171% increase). However, when visibility was high (Study 2), fewer meat substitutes were sold in a pairwise presentation. Higher visibility led to increased sales of meat products, $t(229) = 2.86$, $p = 0.005$, $d = 0.38$.
Positioning The location of sugar sweetened beverages (SSB's) in drink coolers was re-arranged by reducing visibility over a period of 3 weeks. The data collection was supplemented with interviews.	The intervention was able to reduce the purchasing of SSB in three of the four canteens. In one of the canteens where the cooler was behind the cafeteria desk there was a little difference. The total sales numbers of the healthy beverages show an increase of 12%.
Positioning	Positioning fruit and vegetable snack items first and last within an online canteen menu did not increase the selection of these items (OR = 1.136 [95% CI: 0.791, 1.632] $p = 0.490$).
Positioning	The middle options are preferred when food options are displayed horizontally (vs. vertically), whereas the edge items are preferred under a vertical display (vs. a horizontal display). This expectation was confirmed in the χ^2 regression analyses. With respect to the taco choices, preference for the non-edge options was greater under a horizontal display versus a vertical display, both in taco choices: 60.4% (= 58/96) versus 46.2% (= 49/106), $\chi^2 (1) = 4.07$, $p < 0.0$; and in the wine choices: 68.1% (= 62/91) versus 44.1% (= 49/111), $\chi^2 (1) = 11.62$, $p < 0.001$. In study 2, participants' edge avoidance (i.e., preference for the non-edge options in the display) was greater when the options were displayed horizontally versus vertically, 70.9% (= 56/79) versus 55.3% (= 42/76), $\chi^2 (1) = 4.07$, $p < 0.05$.
Positioning	When healthy food products were repositioned at the checkout counter display and unhealthy alternatives remained available elsewhere in the store, the proportion of healthy products in total food sales was higher. An ANOVA analysis revealed a significant effect, $F (1, 54) = 5.20$, $p = 0.027$, $\eta p 2 = 0.09$, such that more products were sold per day during the baseline phase (M = 1594.857, SD = 216.268) than during the nudge phase (M = 1441.321, SD = 283.330). A similar effect was found for the total number

Authors, Year, Journal, Country	Participants
Van Gestel, L. C. et al. *(continue)*	
Keegan, E. et al. 2019 Eating Behaviors Australia	N=143 Undergraduate women were asked to choose a food from a pictorial-style menu that presented a salad and three unhealthier food options in a horizontal line. The position of the salad was manipulated to be presented either (a) in the middle, (b) at the end, or (c) separated by 5 cm to the right of the line of unhealthier food options.
Reijnen, E. et al. 2019 Journal of Consumer Policy Switzerland	N = 45 (Ages 18–62 years of age, M = 32.8; SD = 12.06, 53% female, participants of the Zurich University of Applied Sciences, ZHAW, and the Zurich community). Participants had to choose their most and least preferred cuisine (Italian, Asian, Mexican, Japanese, American) before they completed 5 practice and 42 experimental positioning trials. This resulted in a preference (most/least preferred cuisine) × area (top, middle, bottom) design for each of the three meal types (appetizers, entrées, and desserts).
Charry, K. and Tessitore, T. 2021 Social Science & Medicine United States	N^i = 290 Ages 17–75 (Mage = 34.80; 50% men) The participants were randomly assigned to one of two Twitter pages that were identical except for the number of followers (23 versus 423,000 followers). These pages tweeted about healthy food: one talked about a healthy salad lunch and was accompanied by a picture, and the other mentioned a fresh fruit salad. After watching the assigned Twitter page, participants assessed their healthy eating intentions. N^{ii} = 182 Ages 22–74 years old (M age = 39.3; 55.5% men). The stimuli were identical to those in Study 1. This study measured participants' attitude towards the food presented in the Twitter posts, healthy eating intentions, social value of healthy food, health perception of the food presented on the Twitter page, using a manipulation check of the number of followers, influence of presumed influence, and sociodemographic measures.

Focus area	Key Findings
	of food products sold per day, F $(1, 54) = 4.05$, $p = 0.049$, $\eta p2 = 0.07$, such that more food products were sold during the baseline phase ($M = 751.393$, $SD = 121.332$) than during the nudge phase ($M = 675.714$, $SD = 157.616$).
Positioning	Spatial positioning of healthy and unhealthy food cues affects food choice. The main effects together proved significant, Nagelkerke R2 = 0.09, χ^2 (3) = 7.89, $p = 0.048$, with the middle versus separate term significant, $B = -1.14$, $SE = 0.49$, $p = 0.020$.
Positioning	Appetizers positioned at the top of the menu were chosen more often. Regarding the menus from the most preferred cuisine, participants chose significantly more often entrées in the center of the menu. Regarding desserts, no effects could be found. The effects of the factors of preference and area were tested using the chi-square test for one-way tables. Overall, no significant effects were found for preference, χ^2 (1, N = 1,538) = 0.010, $p = 0.919$, and area, χ^2 (2, N = 1,538) = 3.657, $p = 0.0161$. However, a closer look at the data (single comparisons) showed that in the most preferred condition, participants did choose more dishes from the middle than the top, χ^2 (1, N = 535) = 5.250, $p < 0.05$, and bottom area, χ^2 (1, N = 535) = 7.308, $p < .01$. No such results were found for the least preferred condition (all χ^2 values < 0.124, all p values > 0.725).
Priming	The results showed that a high (versus low) number of followers led to higher healthy eating intentions ($Ms = 3.07$ vs. 2.79; t (288) = -1.81, $p = 0.036$). The participants rated the food presented in the Twitter posts as healthy ($M = 4.52$; $SD = 0.67$). An independent samples t-test showed no difference between the two conditions (t (139) = -0.94; $p = 0.35$) (M High Followers = 4.58; M Low Followers = 4.47).

Authors, Year, Journal, Country	Participants
Wyse, R. et al. 2021 Journal of Medical Internet Research Australia	N = 2207 Students from 17 primary schools with a web-based canteen lunch ordering. The sample was randomized into control (8 schools) and treatment (9 schools) groups.
Starke, A. D. et al. 2021 Frontiers in artificial intelligence Not specified	N = 239 (M age = 32.2 years, SD age = 10.8, 33.3% male)
Bleasdale, J. et al. 2021 Public Health Nutrition United States	N = 179 Participants to a weekly food truck event in Buffalo, New York.
Andersson, O. and Nelander, L. 2021 Games Sweden	N = 7 968 University cafeteria customers in Uppsala
Prusaczyk, E. et al. 2021 Food Quality and Preference Canada	N = 562 Participants were then randomly assigned to the nudge (n = 189), education (n = 187), or control (n = 186) condition, after which they reported their willingness to order an all-beef (vs. beef-mushroom) burger.

Focus area	Key Findings
Priming	The intervention lunch orders had significantly lower energy content (-69.4 kJ, 95% CI -119.6 to -19.1; $p = 0.01$) and saturated fat content (-0.6 g, 95% CI -0.9 to -0.4; $p < 0.001$) than the control lunch orders, but they did not have significantly lower sugar or sodium content. Relative to control schools, intervention schools had significantly greater odds of having everyday items purchased (odds ratio [OR] 1.7, 95% CI 1.5–2.0; $p < 0.001$), corresponding to a 9.8% increase in everyday items, and lower odds of having occasional items purchased (OR 0.7, 95% CI 0.6–0.8; $p < 0.001$), corresponding to a 7.7% decrease in occasional items); however, there was no change in the odds of having caution (least healthy) items purchased (OR 0.8, 95% CI 0.7–1.0; $p = 0.05$).
Priming The study investigated whether healthy food choices can be supported in food search by depicting attractive images alongside recipes, as well as by re-ranking search results using the "traffic light" system of the UK Food Standards Agency (FSA score). Total scores ranged between 4 (=very healthy) and 12 (very unhealthy). The users were asked to search for specific online recipes and to select those they liked the most.	Users tended to choose a healthier recipe if a visually attractive image was depicted alongside it, as well as if it was listed at the top of a list of search results. Accompanying healthy recipes with attractive images and unhealthy recipes with unattractive images decreased the FSA score of chosen recipes (M = 7.46, S.E. = 0.081), compared to recipe lists that depicted baseline images (M = 7.86, S.E. = 0.081): $F(1,238) = 8.34$, $p < 0.01$, $\eta2 = 0.034$.
Priming	Approximately one-third of surveyed participants accepted a healthy sample, with the majority rating the sample positively.
Priming	Placing a vegetarian option instead of a meat option at the top of a menu decreased the share of meat dishes sold by 11% compared to when the vegetarian option was placed at the bottom of the menu and the meat option was placed at the top. This translates to a 6% decrease of CO_2 emissions).
Priming	Nudge and education interventions increased willingness to order beef-mushroom burgers regardless of right-wing ideology or meat-eating attitudes or behaviors.

Authors, Year, Journal, Country	Participants
Blom, Stephanie S. A. H. et al. 2021 Appetite Netherlands	N = 99 (59 female, Mage = 30.70 years old, SDage = 10.90 years) Participants in the high time pressure condition were instructed to do their shopping for a dessert, soda, pasta, and cheese as fast as possible, while participants in the low time pressure condition were told that it did not matter how long they would take for the task. After shopping in the virtual supermarket, they were asked to fill out the questionnaire.
Harbers, M. C. et al. 2021 International Journal of Environmental Research and Public Health Netherlands	N = 15 Adults with low SEP
Rajbhandari-Thapa, J. et al. 2017 Public Health Reports United States	N^i = 842 School nutrition managers and staff members were trained and completed pre- and posttraining surveys. N^{ii} = 325 Managers completed the follow-up survey.
Filimonau, V. and Krivcova, M. 2017 Journal of Cleaner Production United Kingdom	N = 15 Restaurant managers
Sihvonen, J. and Luomala, H. 2017 The International Review of Retail, Distribution and Consumer Research Finland	N = 99 (M = 39.5, SD = 14.2)

Focus area	Key Findings
Priming	There was a significant main effect of nudges, ANOVA: $F_{(1,95)} = 6.41$, $p = 0.013$, $\eta p2 = 0.07$, but no main effect of time pressure, $F_{(1, 95)} = 0.12$, $p = 0.728$, $\eta p2 = 0.00$, nor an interaction effect, $F_{(1, 95)} = 0.644$, $p = 0.424$, $\eta p2 = 0.01$.
Priming	The study identified three physiological determinants of food choice: ill health, hunger and satiety, and taste preferences. Interviewees generally had a positive attitude towards nudges, especially when they were aligned with product preferences, information needs, and beliefs about the food environment. Still, some interviewees also expressed distrust towards nudging strategies, suspecting ulterior motives.
Priming	From pretraining to posttraining, the study found a significant increase in manager and staff member ($n = 842$) knowledge of strategies for enhancing taste perception through the use of creative menu item names (from 78% to 95%, $p < 0.001$) and understanding that food placement in the lunch line influences food selection (from 78% to 95%, $p < 0.001$), and in their self-perceived ability to influence the cafeteria environment (from 91% to 96%, $p < 0.001$). From pretraining to 3-month follow-up, managers ($n = 325$) reported increased use of evidence-based serving strategies: visibility (from 84% to 96% for placing healthy options in >2 locations, $p < 0.001$), convenience (from 63% to 84% for placing plain milk in front of other beverages, $p < 0.001$), sell (from 25% to 38% for branding healthy items with stickers, $p < 0.001$), price (from 17% to 27% for using bundle pricing to encourage sales, $p < 0.001$), and taste (from 77% to 85% for signage demonstrating the benefits of healthy eating, $p = 0.01$).
Priming	This study explores managerial opinions on the role of menu design in shaping more responsible consumer choice. It finds that while restaurateurs acknowledge rising customer awareness about the ramifications of their food choice on personal health and the environment, they are skeptical about the use of menu design as a means to positively affect consumer choice.
Priming	A 4-group between-participants design (health-goal prime vs. responsibility prime vs. status prime vs. no prime) was used. There were product-specific differences between the health-primed and control group for choices of yoghurt ($\chi^2 = 13.89$, $p = 0.003$) and pork cold cuts ($\chi^2 = 7.82$, $p = 0.05$). A health-primed group chose significantly more often the healthy option of yoghurt than the control group did (58.9% vs. 39%). Similarly, the health-primed

Authors, Year, Journal, Country	Participants
Sihvonen, J. and Luomala, H. *(continue)*	
Mai, R. and Hoffmann, S. 2017 Food Quality and Preference Germany	$N^i = 0$ $N^{ii} = 68$ $N^{iii} = 315$ $N^{iiii} = 80$ $N^{iiiii} = 59$ 5 mixed-methods studies that explored the health-supportive side effects of motives that were unrelated to health. Study 1 (qualitative with zero participants) identified quality consciousness and physical appearance consciousness as potential candidates for health-supportive side-effects. Study 2 aimed to unravel how quality and physical appearance are implicitly associated with more or less healthy foods. Study 3 corroborated the side effects of the health-unrelated motives on healthy lifestyles and healthy food consumption. Study 4 and Study 5 externally validated the side effects for actual choices and shopping cart composition.
Kawa, C. et al. 2021 International Journal of Environmental Research and Public Health Germany	N = 904 Students (686) and employees (218) of a German university

Focus area	Key Findings
	group chose lighter pork cold cuts more often than the control group did (26.4% vs. 14.0%).
Priming	Quality consciousness (QC) and physical attractiveness consciousness (PAC) may elicit health-supportive side effects. T-test in Study 2 confirmed that participants pair healthy food more easily with high rather than with low quality (t(33) = 15.33, p < 0.001). All participants pair attractiveness more easily with healthy than with unhealthy food. This effect is highly significant (t(33) = 25.54, p < 0.001). Study 3 showed that QC and PAC impact healthier food-related lifestyles and eating behaviors. For example, PAC fosters eating behaviors in accordance with nutrition guidelines (β = 0.17, p ≤ 0.01). PAC reduces the consumption of deep-frozen convenience foods, fried food, candies, and meat. PAC reduces the BMI, which is a heuristic way to measure of body fatness (β = -0.21, p ≤ 0.001). Yet, unlike QC (β = 0.26, p ≤ 0.001), PAC does not affect the consumption of organic food because organic food is less relevant for weight control. Study 4 confirmed the health-supportive side effects for the consumers' preferences of a healthier product variant. QC (β = 0.24, p < 0.05) and PAC (β = 0.26, p < 0.05) fostered the general consumption of diet food products that was measured with the three-item scale, whereas there is no incremental influence of health consciousness HC (β = 0.04, p > 0.05). At the same time, QC, PAC, and HC drove the actual choice of the reduced-sugar snack bar (QC: B = 1.39, p < 0.01; PAC: B = 1.43, p < 0.05; HC: B = 0.72, p < 0.05). Study 5 revealed that QC (r = 0.34, p < 0.01), PAC (r = 0.28, p < 0.05), and HC (r = 0.33, p < 0.01) were positively related to a healthier composition of the grocery basket. The shopping basket's total calories decreased with elevating levels of QC (r = -0.29, p < 0.05), PAC (r = -0.25, p < 0.05), and HC (r = -0.35, p < 0.01). The analysis also showed very similar patterns for fat (QC: r = -0.20, p = 0.06; PAC: r = 0.23, p < 0.05; HC: r = -0.31, p < 0.01) and carbohydrates (QC: r = -0.29, p < 0.05; PAC: r = 0.18, p = 0.08; HC: r = 0.32, p < 0.01).
Priming The participants were exposed to one out of three nudges while choosing dishes: (1) thin body shape, (2) thick body shape, and (3) the Giacometti artwork nudge.	The Giacometti nudge resulted in more orders for salad among employees. The thin and thick body shape nudges did not change dish orders. For the students, the fourfold chi-squared tests revealed no significant differences regarding the frequency of ordering salad (p = 0.194), fruit salad (p = 0.160) or chocolate pudding (p = 0.869). For the employees, the fourfold chi-squared tests revealed significant differences in the frequency of ordering a salad (χ^2 (3) = 8.570; p = 0.036). Participants in the Giacometti nudge condition ordered 11 more salad dishes than participants in the no-nudge condition, yielding 11.5% more salads ordered considering the total number of salads ordered under all conditions (96 salads).

Authors, Year, Journal, Country	Participants
Tijssen, I. et al. 2017 Food Quality and Preference Netherlands	N^i = 208 (Mean BMI 21.7 ± 1.8 kg/m2), aged between 18 and 45 years old, were divided among two product conditions; the dairy drink (n = 112, 27 male) condition and the sausage (n = 95, 21 male) condition. N^{ii} = 82 (Mean BMI 21.8 ± 1.8 kg/m2) aged between 18 and 45 years old, were selected and divided among 2 product conditions, 36 consumers (n = 9 male) evaluated sweetness, creaminess, fruitiness, and flavor intensity directly after tasting in the dairy drink condition, and 45 consumers (n = 13 male) evaluated saltiness, fattiness, and flavor intensity in the sausage condition.
Stämpfli, A. E. et al. 2017 Appetite Switzerland	N^i = 133 Each participant was given either 20 chocolates (Mweight = 45.21 g, SDweight = 1.32) or 20 blue-berries (Mweight = 39.02 g, SDweight = 4.68). In the cue conditions, a screensaver with thin, human-like sculptures by the artist Alberto Giacometti, running on the laptop computer, was projected on a screen. In the no-cue condi-tions the laptop computer was closed. The direct exposure to the screen during the instructions took about 30 s. After the tasting of either chocolates or blueberries, participants completed a questionnaire.

Focus area	Key Findings
Priming (Investigation of effects of package color cues on expected product properties) 3 color aspects of the package were altered, i.e., hue (dairy drink: blue, purple, red; sausage: blue, green, red), brightness level (high, low), and saturation level (high, low) resulting in 12 package images per product condition.	The participants in Study 1 had stronger associations between package coloring in congruence with regular products and attractiveness and unhealthiness than with unattractiveness and healthiness. For package coloring congruent with healthier alternatives, associations were stronger with unattractiveness and healthiness than vice versa. Faster response latencies were seen when healthy terms were combined with pictures of packages representing healthier alternatives (dairy drink mean: 849.ms; sausage mean: 946.70ms) compared to the combination of unhealthy terms and pictures representing healthy alternatives (dairy drink mean: 1053.90; sausage mean: 994.51 ms). Red package color (hue) created the highest expectations for sweetness, creaminess (dairy drink), fattiness (sausage) and flavor intensity (both products). Decreasing color brightness increased expected sweetness intensity. Increasing brightness increased expected flavor intensity for the dairy drink but decreased expected flavor intensity for the sausage. Increasing color saturation increased expected sweetness (dairy drink) and expected flavor intensity (both products). Especially combining red hue with low brightness and/or high saturation boosted expectations. Study 2 showed that hue significantly affected the dairy drinks' creaminess perception ($F(1,245) = 5.00$, $p = 0.03$) where red hue (a warmer color) scored lower on creaminess perception compared to blue hue (a cooler color). Increasing brightness significantly decreased the sausages' perceived fattiness ($F(1,308) = 4.50$, $p = 0.05$) and flavor intensity ($F(1,308) = 3.91$, $p = 0.05$) while it increased dairy drinks' creaminess perception ($F(1,245) = 4.72$, $p = 0.03$). Increasing saturation increased the dairy drinks' sweetness perception ($F(1,245) = 5.01$, $p = 0.03$).
Priming	The participants in Study 1 rated the food samples to be healthier when they tasted blueberries (M = 5.77, SD = 1.33) than when they tasted chocolates (M = 2.74, SD = 1.25), $t(111) = 12.48$, $p < 0.001$, d = 2.35. Food healthiness did not influence the Giacometti effect, $F(1, 110) = 0.20$, $p = 0.66$, $\eta^2 = 0.00$. Regarding the type of food, the ANOVA revealed a main effect of food healthiness, $F(1, 110) = 11.58$, $p < 0.001$, $\eta^2 = 0.09$.

Authors, Year, Journal, Country	Participants
Stämpfli, A. E. et al. *(continue)*	N^{ii} =71 The Giacometti cue (see Study 1) was presented as a screensaver directly on participants' computers before they started the computer-based questionnaire. In the no-cue condition, the computers showed a static, white screen. The participants had been assigned the word completion task before they completed the questionnaire.
Filimonau et al. 2017 Journal of Cleaner Production United Kingdom	N = 340 Restaurant visitors
Peng-Li, D. et al. 2020 Food Quality and Preference China, Denmark	N = 72 Participants (37 Chinese, 35 Danish) were each exposed to three sound conditions (sweet music [SwM], salty music [SaM], no music [NoM]) while observing different food items in a choice paradigm.
Allan, J. L., and Powell, D. J. 2020 International Journal of Behavioral Nutrition and Physical Activity United Kingdom	N = 30 (15 intervention, 15 control) Hospital shops in Scotland were tested whether a Point of Purchase Prompt (PPP) could reduce the average calorie, fat and/or sugar content of purchased snacks for a 12-week baseline and 12-week follow-up period.

Focus area	Key Findings
	In Study 2, the Giacometti sculptures in increased the weight-related word completion of restrained eaters. One-factor ANOVAs revealed no effect of the Giacometti screensaver on the amount of weight-related, $F(1, 59) < 0.01$, $p = 0.99$, $\eta^2 = 0.00$, or health-related words mentioned, $F(1, 59) = 0.71$, $p = 0.40$, $\eta^2 = 0.01$.
Priming	80.5% of respondents paid close attention and considered the information presented before placing a food order. While price represented an important factor in customer decision-making ($M = 2.56$, where 1 = strongly agree and 5 = strongly disagree), there were more influential determinants of consumer choice, such as provenance of ingredients ($M = 2.39$; and the food nutritional values (amounts of fat, including saturated fat, salt, and sugar) ($M = 2.42$).
Priming	Across both cultures, participants spent more time fixating on sweet food while listening to "sweet music" and salty food when listening to "salty music", while no differences were observed in the no music condition. Danish participants had, regardless of sound condition, longer fixation times on the food images compared to their Chinese counterparts. Participants 'choices in each sound condition were consistent with fixation time spent, implying a clear congruency effect between music and choice behavior. The chi-square tests showed participants choose significantly sweeter food items during the SwM condition compared the NoM condition (proportion of SwM = 59.03% vs. proportion of NoM = 52.08%, $\chi^2 (1) = 11.13$, $p < 0.001$), and significantly saltier food items during the SaM condition compared the NoM condition (proportion of SaM = 52.95% vs. proportion of NoM = 47.92%, $\chi^2 (1) = 5.85$, $p = 0.016$). Likewise, significantly sweeter food choices (vs. salty food choices) were made in the SwM compared to the SaM condition $(\chi^2 (1) = 16.12$, $p < 0.001$.
Priming	Point of Purchase Prompt (PPP—a sign displayed at eye level on shop shelves—designed to prompt purchasers to choose a healthier snack at the moment of choice can produce small but statistically significant reductions in the energy content of snack purchases from hospital shops. Data from over 1 million snack purchases were analyzed. Snacks purchased from intervention sites were, on average, significantly lower in calorie ($\gamma = -1.84$, $p < 0.001$) and sugar ($\gamma = -0.18$, $p = 0.030$) at the follow-up relative to baseline, but only the reduction in calories was significantly different to control. Average expenditure per item also reduced significantly in intervention (but not control) sites ($\gamma = -0.89$, $p < 0.001$). The intervention had no effect on the fat content of snacks, or the number of snacks sold.

Authors, Year, Journal, Country	Participants
Lange, C. et al. 2020 Appetite France	N = 171 Children (ages 7–11) were asked to imagine the taste, smell, and texture of eating palatable foods, i.e., chocolate cereal, chocolate waffle, and chocolate candies. Children were then asked to choose between the recommended serving size, a 50% larger portion, and a 125% larger portion of either brownie or applesauce. One week later, they were placed in the same condition for the other food.
Erjavec, M. et al. 2020 European Journal of Clinical Nutrition United Kingdom	N = 107 Children's lunchtime consumption was measured in 2 primary schools directly through the use of a validated digital photography protocol. Measures were taken at baseline and again after a 3-week long intervention.
Sharps, M. A. et al., 2019 Digital Health United Kingdom	N^i = 20 (Undergraduate students, mean age = 19) N^{ii} = 44 (23 intervention, 21 control condition) (Adolescents, mean age = 14.4) Two pilot interventions examined whether exposure to images of peers' portions of high-energy-dense (HED). Snacks and sugar-sweetened beverages (SSBs) on social media (Instagram) would influence reported desired portion sizes.
McAlister, A. R. et al. 2020 Health Communication United States	N = 140 (College students at a large Midwestern university in the US, 76% women) Instances when participants consumed a snack and correctly reported that they did were coded as 0, meaning correct reporting. Instances when participants did not consume a snack while reporting that they did were labeled as overreporting.

Focus area	Key Findings
Priming	Food sensory imagery may be a useful intervention to nudge children towards healthier portion size choices because it reduces the selected portion size of an energy-dense snack without reducing the selected portion size of a healthier snack. The study with the two foods together (brownie, applesauce) revealed that hungrier children (B - 0.03, t (163) - 3.21, p < 0.01) and heavier children (B = 0.04, t (163) = 2.04, p < 0.05) chose significantly larger portions. Moreover, children chose significantly larger portions for brownie than for applesauce (B = -0.37, t (163) = -7.94, p < 0.01). There was no significant interaction between imagery and real conditions (p = 0.65).
Priming	Changes to the choice architecture of dining rooms (e.g., improved presentation and provision of target foods, attractive advertisements, labeling, prompting by staff) resulted in increase in consumption of fruit with the schoolchildren, but their selection of vegetables did not change or even declined. For children who took school lunches (n = 67), both selection and consumption of fruit increased as the result of the intervention (z = -4.692, p < 0.001, 110 r = -0.74 and z = -3.950, p < 0.001, r = -0.48 respectively). No changes were observed in the comparison group (n = 40), who brought their lunch boxes from home.
Priming	Exposure to images of peers' portions of high-energy-dense (HED) snacks and sugar-sweetened beverages (SSBs) on social media (Instagram) reduced desired portion sizes of HED snacks and SSBs in young adults, but not in adolescents. Intervention 1: there was a significant main effect of time (F (1, 19) = 14.68, p = 0.001, ηp^2 = 0.44). Participants reported smaller desired portion sizes of HED snacks and SSBs at intervention end than at baseline. There was no significant food type by time interaction (F (1, 19) = 3.70, p = 0.07, ηp^2 = 0.16) on participants' desired portion sizes of HED snacks and SSBs between baseline and intervention end. Intervention 2: there was no significant main effect of condition (F (1, 41) = 0.92, p = 0.34, ηp^2 = 0.02), no significant main effect of time (F (1, 41) = 0.58, p = 0.45, ηp^2 = 0.01) and no significant interactions (p > 0.05). Thus, the intervention did not influence participants to reduce their desired portion sizes of HED snacks or SSBs relative to the control condition.
Priming	People sometimes eat greater amounts of preferred foods than they realize when they are multitasking with screen devices. By surrounding oneself with snack-size fruits, vegetables, and nuts in multitasking situations, mindless eating could be a powerful nudge to facilitate greater consumption of preferred foods to combat health concerns. The interaction effect of media use and snack type on over-reporting was not significant, F (3,132) = 1.59, p = 0.194, ηp^2 = 0.04. However, the interaction effect of media use and snack type on under-reporting was significant, F (3,132) = 2.69, p = 0.049, ηp^2 = 0.06.

Authors, Year, Journal, Country	Participants
McAlister, A. R. et al. *(continue)*	Instances when participants consumed a snack while reporting they did not, were considered to be underreporting.
Boehm, R. et al. 2020 Public Health Nutrition United States	The data included 332 school days across the 3 schools (The Healthy Choices, Healthy Nudging and Comparison Schools, 282 baseline days; 50 intervention days). The study aimed to compare federally reimbursable school meals served when competitive foods were removed and when marketing and nudging strategies were used in school cafeterias operating the National School Lunch Program (NSLP). The second objective was to determine how marketing and nudging strategies influenced competitive food sales.
Walker, L. A. et al. 2019 Royal Society Open Science United Kingdom	Evidence-based recommendations for public health policy to combat obesity. On average, 26% of UK adults classify as obese double the global average.
Tangari, A. H., Banerjee, S., and Verma, S. 2019 Journal of Business Research United States	N^i =112 Respondents (39% female, mean age = 25) were presented with an ad for a milk product as the healthy product or with an ad for a cola product as the unhealthy product.

Focus area	Key Findings
	Pairwise comparisons (Bonferroni) indicated participants significantly underreported their consumption of preferred snacks (M = 0.68, SD = 0.76) over EDNP (Energy-Dense, Nutrient-Poor) snacks—M&Ms, sugar candy, potato chips—(M = 0.27, SD = 0.51) in three-screen multitasking, TV + texting + shopping, condition (higher numbers indicated greater under-reporting) (p = 0.003). Under-reporting of preferred snack selection was also significantly higher in the TV + texting + shopping than TV + texting condition (M = 0.25, SD = 0.44; p = 0.043).
Priming	Removing competitive foods, marketing, and nudging may increase school meal participation. Yet, there was no evidence that promoting school meals decreased competitive food sales. This suggests that an increase in meal participation may not necessarily be associated with a decrease in competitive food purchases. Estimated Difference-in-Differences (DID) values for all outcome measures show that the number of daily entrées served was significantly higher in the Healthy Choices and Healthy Nudging Schools during the intervention period relative to the Comparison School. In the Healthy Nudging School, the average number of daily hot and cold entrées were both significantly higher during the intervention period. In the Healthy Choices School, the average number of cold entrées served, as well as the proportion of entrées served with vegetables were significantly higher during the intervention compared with the Comparison School. In the Healthy Nudging School, there were no significant changes in meal component selection or total number of competitive foods sold.
Priming	Dietary-choice interventions made by modifying the food environment have been shown to be effective in tackling obesity. However, this type of intervention is typically challenging for policymakers to implement for economic, ethical, and public accessibility reasons. To overcome these concerns, policymakers should consider 'boosting' interventions. Boosting involves enhancing competences that help people make decisions consistent with their goals.
Priming	Using claim congruency—adding a health message to the promotional claim that is aligned with the product related cue—can nudge more positive attitudes and purchase intentions. No effect of the ultrafunctional message for the unhealthy product was observed. Study 1: ad attitude Adatt ($F_{(1, 108)}$ = 4.47, p < 0.05) and purchase intentions ($F_{(1, 108)}$ = 4.15, p < 0.05). The healthy product Adatt ($F_{(1, 108)}$ = 5.49, p < 0.05) and purchase intentions ($F_{(1, 108)}$ = 8.57, p < 0.005) were higher for the ad for the healthy product with the ultrafunctional claim (MAdatt = 4.80, Mpurchase intentions = 3.89) than for the control ad for the healthy product (MAdatt = 3.80, Mpurchase intentions = 2.60).

Authors, Year, Journal, Country	Participants
Tangari, A. H., Banerjee, S. and Verma, S. *(continue)*	N^{ii} = 200 Participants (41% female, mean age = 34) were presented with an ad for a granola bar as a healthy product and a chocolate candy bar as an unhealthy product. N^{iii} = 232 Respondents from business school classes in the US consisting of full-time and part-time nontraditional students (60% male, mean age = 24) were presented with an ad for a granola bar as a healthy product and a chocolate candy bar as an unhealthy product. N^{iiii} = 136 Participants from Arizona Mechanical (38% female, mean age = 33) were presented with an ad for cola as an unhealthy product.
Tonkin, M. et al. 2019 Appetite Australia	N = 210 (18–32, M = 21.57, SD = 3.33) Participants were presented with a pictorial café-style menu displaying a healthy food cue (basket of fruit and vegetables) either on the menu cover or inside the menu, or they received a control menu. Participants were then asked to make one choice from each of three menu sections (meals, beverages, afters) and to complete a measure of dietary restraint.

Focus area	Key Findings
	Study 2: ad attitude Adatt ($F_{(1, 196)} = 5.67$, $p < 0.02$) and purchase intentions ($F_{(1, 196)} = 11.83$, $p < .01$). The ad making the healthy ultrafunctional claim had more positive Adatt ($M = 5.15$) and stronger purchase intentions ($M = 4.81$) than the control ad for the healthy product ($M_{Adatt} = 4.23$; $F_{(1, 196)} = 10.53$), $p < 0.01$; and $M_{purchase\ intentions} = 3.84$; $F_{(1, 196)} = 10.04$ $p < 0.01$). The addition of an ultrafunctional claim had no impact on the taste goal for the unhealthy product ($F_{(1, 98)} = 2.14$, $p > 0.10$). For the healthy product there was not a significant interaction between the ad claim condition and the product goal condition ($F < 1$) nor was there an effect of the ad claim condition for the healthy product ($F < 1$). Study 3: Adatt ($F_{(1, 228)} = 3.94$, $p < 0.05$) and purchase intentions ($F_{(1, 228)} = 5.11$, $p < 0.05$). The ad for the unhealthy product with the ultrafunctional claims plus health message resulted in more positive purchase intentions ($M = 4.32$) and a marginally more positive Adatt ($M = 4.58$) than the ad that did not include a health message ($M_{purchase\ intentions} = 3.56$, $F_{(1, 228)} = 5.19$, $p < 0.05$ and $M_{Adatt} = 4.05$; $F_{(1, 228)} = 3.04$, $p = 0.08$). There was no effect of the ad claim condition for the healthy product (p's > 0.20). For the unhealthy product, the taste goal was significantly stronger ($M = 5.63$) compared to the health goal ($M = 4.86$) when presented with the ultrafunctional product claim ($p < 0.02$). Study 4: The health goal was stronger in the ultrafunctional claim condition ($M = 3.76$) than for the control condition ($M = 2.41$; $p < 0.001$).
Priming	The timing of presentation of a healthy food cue is critical. The participants made more healthy food choices when the healthy cue was presented before, on the menu cover. Food choices were analyzed by a 3 menu conditions: healthy cue before, healthy cue simultaneous, control cue x 2 (dietary restraint status: restrained, unrestrained) between-subjects ANOVA. There was a significant main effect of menu condition, $F_{(2, 209)} = 21.36$, $p < 0.001$, $\eta^2 = 0.171$. Participants assigned to the healthy-cue-before menu condition made significantly more healthy food and beverage choices ($M = 64.75$, $SD = 31.54$) than did those assigned to the healthy-cue-simultaneous menu condition ($M = 40.47$, $SD = 30.50$), $p < 0.001$, $d = 0.78$, and the control-cue menu condition ($M = 31.42$, $SD = 31.53$), $p < 0.001$, $d = 1.05$, with large effect sizes. Healthy choices did not differ between the latter two menu conditions, $p = 0.259$, $d = 0.29$. There was no main effect of dietary restraint status on food choice, $F_{(1, 209)} = 2.44$, $p = 0.120$, $\eta^2 = 0.009$. Restrained eaters ($M = 48.76$, $SD = 37.14$) did not make significantly more healthy food choices than did unrestrained eaters ($M = 42.15$, $SD = 30.37$). However, there was a significant interaction between menu condition and dietary restraint status, $F_{(2, 209)} = 4.04$, $p = 0.019$, $\eta^2 = 0.031$.

Authors, Year, Journal, Country	Participants
Zhou, X. et al. 2019 Food Quality and Preference Denmark, France, Italy, and the United Kingdom	N = 97 Urban dwellers aged 65 years and above from four European countries (Denmark, France, Italy, and the United Kingdom)
Saulais, L. et al. 2019 Food policy France	N = 294 (Consumers of a self-service restaurant) Participants chose between a target vegetable-based dish (vg1) and one, or two alternatives: a meat-based dish (nvg) and another vegetable dish (vg2).
Rogus, S. 2018 Appetite United States	N = 4826 (Households) USDA's National Household Food Acquisition and Purchase Survey was used to examine the relationship between time constraints (objective and perceived) and HEI-2010 score of food purchases and examines this relationship by income.

Focus area	Key Findings
Priming	Nudging by 'dish-of-the-day' (veggie balls) did not influence older people's dish choice (veggie balls, meatballs, or fish cakes). Participants from the UK and Denmark were more likely to choose the plant-based dish when compared with participants from France. Security and universalism were found significantly related to the participants 'plant-based dish choice. Cronbach's alpha for Security was 0.57 and for universalism was 0.63. The security score and participants' plant-based dish choice showed a reverse association while universalism score and the same dish choice presented a positive relationship. For the security dimension, participants with higher scores were 30% less likely to choose the plant-based dish. Regarding the universalism dimension, participants with higher scores were 65.8% more likely to choose the plant-based option. Compared with females, males were 47.4% less likely to choose the plant-based dish. When France was defined as reference, the United Kingdom and Denmark had a 198.7% and 173.2% higher likelihood of choosing the plant-based dish, respectively.
Priming	The "Dish-of-the-day" nudge (DoD effect) led to an increase in relative choice of the target dish. The DoD effect was greater for less popular dishes and increased with the number of options. 5 choice task conditions were tested: three conditions examined dish choices when two options were available (vg1 versus nvg): no DoD (T1-0); vg1 as DoD (T1a); or nvg as DoD (T1b). 2 further conditions used three options (vg1 versus nvg versus vg2): no nudge (T2-0), or vg1 as DoD (T2a). In neutral conditions T1-0 and T2-0 respectively, 34.4% and 23.3% of consumers chose vg1. The DoD effect was observed in all conditions: choices in favor of vg1 increased by 25.2% when in was DoD by 25.2% in T1a vs. T1-0 and by 30% in T2a vs. T2-0; while 7.6% more consumers chose nvg in T1b vs. T1-0. Regarding the conditions of DoD effectiveness, the size of the DoD effect was larger for the initially less popular dish vg1 compared with nvg. Introducing more options also increased the relative effect of DoD in favor of vg1, from 73% to 129%. There were no effects of the condition on consumer satisfaction with the dish chosen, nor on the amount of food wasted.
Priming	Perceived time constraint lowers Healthy Eating Index (HEI) Score of food purchases for higher-income households, or for those between 400% and 600% of the poverty line but for not low-income households. Having a higher income to poverty ratio was associated with a decrease in the expected HEI score of household food purchases where the food shopper felt time-constrained (-0.06, $p = 0.059$).

Authors, Year, Journal, Country	Participants
Rowley, J. and Spence, C. 2018 Appetite United Kingdom	N^i = 122 N^{ii} = 124 The studies assessed how the placing (i.e., visual composition) of a dish influences people's hedonic preference and their perception of portion size.

Focus area	Key Findings
Priming	The plate of food was rated as constituting a larger portion when the elements were arrayed-horizontally rather than stacked vertically. The centrally placed dessert was rated as a larger portion than the offset version of the exact same dish. The food was also liked more and the participants/diners were willing to pay more for it when arranged horizontally and/or centrally.
	Experiment 1: Estimated portion size: the analysis revealed a significant difference in estimated portion size [$F(1, 122) = 83.81$, $p < .001$, partial $\eta^2 = 0.41$], with the horizontally arrayed plating arrangement rated as containing significantly more food ($M = 5.56$, $SE = 0.157$; with a rating of 7 being 'huge' and 1 as 'tiny') than the vertically stacked arrangement ($M = 3.39$, $SE = 0.179$).
	Liking: The participants liked the horizontally arrayed food significantly more than the vertically stacked arrangement ($M = 4.82$, $SE = 0.173$ vs. $M = 2.95$, $SE = 0.171$) [$F(1, 122) = 59.13$, $p < 0.001$, partial $\eta^2 = 0.33$]. WTP: The participants were willing to pay (WTP) significantly more for the food when it was arrayed-horizontally on the plate ($M = \$5.31$, $SE = \$0.24$) that when stacked vertically ($M = \$3.29$, $SE = \$0.27$) [$F(1, 122) = 30.42$, $p < 0.001$, partial $\eta2 = 0.20$]. Artistic value: There was no significant difference in terms of ratings of how artistic the horizontally arrayed vs. vertically stacked plates of food looked [$F(1, 122) = 0.362$, $p = 0.58$].
	Experiment 2: Estimated portion size: with starters, there was a significant effect of visual arrangement on estimated portion size [$F(1, 122) = 4.04$, $p = 0.05$, partial $\eta2 = 0.18$], with the diners once again rating the vertically stacked starter as constituting a smaller portion ($M = 2.77$, $SE = 0.075$) than the horizontally arrayed version of exactly the same elements ($M = 3.19$, $SE = 0.075$). With desserts, the analysis revealed a significant effect of visual arrangement on estimated portion size [$F (1, 122) = 31.57$, $p < 0.001$, partial $\eta2 = 0.45$], with diners rating the centrally presented dessert as larger ($M = 3.29$, $SE = 0.131$) than the offset presentation ($M = 2.31$, $SE = 0.116$). Liking: With starters, there was a significant effect of visual arrangement on liking [$F (1, 122) = 68.62$, $p < 0.001$, partial $\eta2 = 0.60$], with the diners liking the visual arrangement of the horizontally arrayed starter more ($M = 4.82$, $SE = 0.172$) than the vertically presented version ($M = 2.92$, $SE = 0.127$). With desserts, the analysis revealed a significant effect of visual arrangement on liking [$F(1, 122) = 49.21$, $p < 0.001$, partial $\eta2 = 0.54$], with diners preferring the visual arrangement of the centrally presented dessert course more ($M = 4.18$, $SE = 0.096$) than the offset dessert ($M = 2.92$, $SE = 0.151$). WTP: With starters, there was significant effect of visual arrangement on WTP [$F (1, 122) = 68.16$, $p < 0.001$, partial $\eta2 = 0.60$], with diners being willing to pay more for the horizontally arrayed starter ($M = £6.46$, $SD = £1.86$) than for exactly the same food when stacked vertically ($M = £3.34$, $SD = £2.22$).

Authors, Year, Journal, Country	Participants
Rowley, J. and Spence, C. *(continue)*	
Wan, X., Qiu, L., and Wang, C. 2021 Applied Psychology: Health and Well-Being China	N = 52 (Mean age = 20.85 ± 1.88 years; 28 females) The study examined how the color contrast between the food and the background might influence people's choices between meat and vegetable dishes. Participants were instructed to choose three desirable dishes out of a choice set presented on a red- or green-colored table in a simulated restaurant environment.
Bacon, L. and Krpan, D. 2018 Appetite United Kingdom	N = 853 (UK resident adults, 453 female) Participants were presented one of the four randomly assigned menus and were asked to select a main course they would have for dinner.
Dos Santos, Q. et al. 2018 International Journal of Consumer Studies Denmark	N = 191 94 adolescents (aged 10–19 years) and 97 older people (aged ≥65 years) were asked to choose between three similar meals, one meat, one fish and one VeggiEat dish. The VeggiEat dish was labelled the "Dish of the Day."
Carroll, K. A. et al. 2018 Appetite United States	N = 367 Participants were recruited for a single session each lasting approximately 60 min; on average 9–16 participants were present for any individual session. Participants were recruited through advertisements in local newspapers, online community bulletin boards, at local community centers, public libraries, and at grocery stores within a 20-min driving radius to the college campus of the University of Wisconsin-Madison.

Focus area	Key Findings
	With desserts, the analysis revealed a significant effect $[F (1, 122) = 6.517, p = 0.012,$ partial $\eta 2 = 0.23]$, with diners willing to pay more for the centrally placed dessert ($M = £5.75$, $SD = £2.64$) than for exactly the same food when offset ($M = £4.81, SD = £2.54$). Artistic value: With starters, the analysis revealed a significant effect of visual arrangement on artistic value $[F (1, 122) = 24.46, p < 0.001,$ partial $\eta 2 = 0.41]$, with diners rating the vertically stacked starter ($M = 3.15, SE = 0.120$) as looking significantly more artistic than when the same food was arrayed horizontally instead ($M = 2.29, SE = 0.120$). With desserts, the analysis revealed a significant effect of visual arrangement on artistic value $[F (1, 122) = 20.44, p < 0.001,$ partial $\eta 2 = 0.38]$, with diners rating the offset dessert ($M = 3.60, SE = 0.188$) as looking significantly more artistic than the same food elements when presented centrally ($M = 2.53, SE = 0.145$).
Priming	The participants chose the meat-heavy meals more often. However, using a red table to present the choice set shifted them toward choosing fewer meat-heavy meals and thus more vegetable-forward meals. The meat dishes looked less attractive when presented on the red tables than on the green tables, $t (51) = 2.42, p = 0.038,$ Cohen's $d = 0.34$, whereas the vegetable dishes looked comparably attractive when presented on the red and green tables, $t (51) = 1.69, p = 0.20$.
Priming	The recommendation menu (Odds Ratio = 1.104, 95% CI [0.618, 1.973], $p = 0.738$) and descriptive menu (Odds Ratio = 0.917, 95% CI [0.503, 1.673], $p = 0.779$) increased the likelihood of vegetarian dish choices for infrequent eaters of vegetarian foods, whereas these effects tended to reverse for frequent vegetarians (Odds Ratio = 0.406, 95% CI [0.195, 0.848], $p = 0.016$).
Priming	"The dish of the day" seems not to work for Danish adolescents and elderly population. The dish choices showed no differences between the control and intervention groups in both age groups, and no differences were found among the other variables analyzed.
Priming	Displayed bundles of fruit and vegetables (F&Vs.) may increase purchasing. There was a significant interaction between cognitive loads and price discounting. The highest percentage of F&Vs. is selected when participants are under no cognitive load and view discounted bundles: 63.51% of these selections contain F&V items. In contrast, when participants view discounted bundles under high cognitive load, the lowest percentage of F&Vs. (48.19%) and the highest percentage of junk food items (23.3%) are selected. When non-discounted bundles were displayed, a 5.86% increase in F&V items was observed compared to Control, although not statistically significant.

Authors, Year, Journal, Country	Participants
Carroll, K. A. et al. *(continue)*	
Grutzmacher, S. K. et al. 2018 Journal of Hunger and Environmental Nutrition United States	N = 972 Using data from parents of low-income elementary school children enrolled in Text2BHealthy. Participants received SMS text messages including nutrition, physical activity stop messages (i.e., messages with instructions how to drop out) and other topics.
Lai, C. Y., List, J. A., and Samek, A, 2020 American Journal of Agricultural Economics United States	A field experiments in a school lunchroom with 2,500 children, evaluating the impact of informational prompts on milk choice and consumption over two weeks.
Mohr, B. et al. 2019 Appetite Germany	N = 401 (University students) Before starting to order, participants were asked to indicate their calorie goal.
Muñoz- Vilches, N. C., van Trijp, H. C. M., and Piqueras-Fiszman, B. 2019 Food Quality and Preference Netherlands	N = 76 (52 females and 24 males, ages 18–45) Participants were allocated to two mental simulation conditions and were told to imagine consuming or having consumed a vice and a virtue product. After imagining each product, the participants rated their level of wanting and indicated the product they preferred: the vice or the virtue one.

Focus area	Key Findings
	Displaying discounted bundles compared to Control resulted in a 14.87% increase (p = 0.0003) in F&V selection, a 3.06% decrease (p = 0.0628) in Junk Food/Snack Items, and an 11.79% decrease (p = 0.0007) in Protein/Dairy/Grain Items. Displaying discounted bundles resulted in 9.01% more (p = 0.0584) F&V items compared to when non-discounted bundles were displayed.
Priming	Text2BHealthy (a text message program) significantly encourages improved nutrition and physical practices of parents and their children. Receiving a stop message increased the probability of attrition compared with receiving. messages about nutrition, physical activity, or other topics (hazard ratio = 51.5, 95% CI 32.46–81.7; p < 0.001). Furthermore, each additional stop message received increased the probability of attrition (hazard ratio = 10.36, 95% CI 6.14–17.46; p < 0.001). The degree of rurality also had a significant effect on the probability of attrition, with metropolitan county participants more likely to drop out of the program than rural county participants. The interaction between SMS text message type and total number of stop messages received had a significant effect on attrition, with the effect of the number of stop messages received dependent on the SMS text message tye. Receiving a stop message increased the probability of dropping out compared with receiving messages about nutrition, physical activity, or other topics (hazard ratio = 51.5, 95% CI 32.46–81.7; p < 0.001). Furthermore, each additional stop message received increased the probability of dropping out (hazard ratio = 10.36, 95% CI 6.14–17.46; p < 0.001).
Priming	Prompts increased the consumption of healthier white milk relative to sugar-sweetened chocolate milk in a school lunchroom from 20% in the control group to 30% in the treatment groups. Adding health or taste messaging did not seem to make a difference. The prompts were nearly as effective as a small nonmonetary incentive.
Priming	Indicating the calorie goal before the purchase leads to significantly fewer calories in the fast-food order (by 106.27 kcal) The effect is due to women ordering fewer high-calorie dishes (women were found to order 119.61 kcal fewer compared to men) Men, in contrast, are unresponsive to changes in the choice context regarding calories ordered.
Priming	Instructed mental simulation has potential to nudge people towards healthier choices. There was no significant main effect of mental simulation on wanting $F_{(2,150)} = 1.66$, p = 0.193, but a significant main effect of product type $F_{(1, 75)} = 19.46$, p < 0.0001. Simulation of imagining the moment of consumption enhanced wanting and choosing the vice product. Simulation of post-consumption enhanced wanting for, and choice of the virtue product.

Authors, Year, Journal, Country	Participants
Sogari, G. et al. 2019 Nutrients United States	N = 3,734 (The study was conducted in a large US college dining venue during lunch).
Djupegot, I.L. 2019 British Food Journal Norway	N = 184 (University students) N° = 41 (Pretested in source credibility (high vs. low)) N°° = 66 (Pre-tested in argument strength) A 2 × 2 scenario-based between-subjects factorial experiment with source credibility (high vs. low) and argument strength (high vs. low) as factors were applied.
Anzman-Frasca, S. et al. 2018 Physiology and Behavior United States	N = 58 Families with children ages 4–8 recruited from a location with Anderson's Frozen Custard, a local quick-service restaurant chain. Families were randomly assigned to return to the restaurant during an intervention or control period. During the intervention period families received free meals and also received placemats featuring two healthy "Kids' Meals of the Day" upon restaurant entry.

Focus area	Key Findings
Priming	Psychological health claims (i.e., rich in B vitamins, which help to reduce fatigue) of whole grains seem more attractive than physiological health claims (i.e., maintaining a healthy weight). Most diners chose tortellini (n = 1325) and spinach fettuccine (n = 992), followed by white and whole grain penne. 725 and 692 diners selected the white penne (19.4%) and the whole grain penne (18.5%), respectively. The Wilcoxon nonparametric paired tests showed that labeling whole grain penne with the vitamin message resulted in a 7.4% higher probability of selecting this pasta than the no-message condition (p < 0.001) and 6% higher than the fiber message condition (p < 0.001). No significant difference was observed between the fiber message and the selection of whole grain penne. The results also show that when presented with the vitamin message for whole grain penne, the percentage of diners who chose spinach fettuccine decreased by 4% relative to the percentage of diners who chose spinach fettuccine when no message was presented (p < 0.05). The probability of choosing spinach fettuccine is not significantly different than choosing whole grain penne when presented with the vitamin message (p = 0.482). These effects were not observed for tortellini pasta, with its frequency remaining stable across treatment.
Priming	Argument strength had a positive main effect on the perceived effectiveness of nudging and there was a significant positive interaction effect of source credibility vs. argument strength on the perceived effectiveness of nudging. The study tested 3 hypotheses: H1 suggested a positive main effect of source credibility on the perceived effectiveness of textual information about food-related nudging, but this was not supported ($F(1, 180) = 0.936$, $p = 0.335$). H2 suggested a positive main effect of argument strength on the perceived effectiveness of textual information about food-related nudging, and this was supported ($F(1, 180) = 5.295$, $p = 0.023$). Finally, H3 suggested a positive interaction effect of source credibility and argument strength on the perceived effectiveness of textual information about food-related nudging. This was supported, although the effect was only borderline significant ($F(1, 180) = 4.054$, $p = 0.046$).
Priming	Children who were exposed to the study placemats presenting healthy food ordered a significantly greater number of healthy food components (p = 0.03). Overall, in the intervention group, 21% of children ordered a healthy entrée or side dish, versus 7% of controls. Children who ordered one of the promoted healthy entrées consumed less saturated fat across the total meal compared to those who did not (p = 0.04).

Authors, Year, Journal, Country	Participants
Mors, M. R. et al. 2018 Food Quality and Preference Netherlands	N = 37 (Age 21–55 years) Participants took part in three sessions: two priming conditions (bread and cucumber odor) and one control condition (no odor).
Stamos, A. et al. 2018 Frontiers in Psychology Belgium, Greece	N = 115 (77% female, M_{age} = 27.55, SD = 9.45) The study was held in two different university labs (in Belgium and Greece). The participants received either two bowls of peanut M&M's (600g per bowl) or two bowls of Maltesers (400g per bowl) in Belgium (depending on their preference) and two bowls Maltesers in Greece (200g per bowl).
Immink, V. et al. 2021 International Journal of Workplace Health Management Netherlands	N^i = 136 meetings N^{ii} = 88 meetings N^{iii} = 88 meetings The main objective was to examine the effect that making vegetable snacks available at workplace meetings would have on consumption. The attendees were exposed to an assortment of vegetables, varying in vegetable variety and presence of promotional leaflet in study 1, serving container in study 2 and additional presence of cookies in study 3.
Grebitus, C. et al. 2020 Journal of Cleaner Production United States	N^i = 109 (M_{age} = 22 years, SD = 5.7, 37.6% female) Study 1 took place in a laboratory setting. N^{ii} = 208 (M_{age} = 44 years, SD = 16.6, 57.4% female) Study 2 took place online. Participants were randomly assigned to complete their choice and search tasks either with pro-environmental nudge messaging (Environmental Condition) or without any guidance (Unguided Condition).
Knowles, D. et al. 2019 Appetite United Kingdom	N = 56 Participants were asked to complete a two-part questionnaire under the cover story of a relaxation study. Two bowls were presented to participants, each containing either 250 g chocolate M&M's or 250 g mixed fruit pieces. Each bowl was positioned either 20 cm or 70 cm from the participant, creating four proximity conditions. Consumption of each snack was compared between proximity conditions.

Focus area	Key Findings
Priming	Odor priming and control conditions did not affect lunch selections (χ^2 (2, N = 37) = 28.1, p = 0.46). However, self-reported positive mood was significantly affected by odor condition (F (2, 72) = 3.26, p = 0.044).
Priming	Consumption of tempting food is decreased after exposure to tempting food cues in a context of a task that discourages food consumption in healthy-weight but not in obese-weight individuals. A significant interaction of weight status and the pre-exposure manipulation emerged [F (1,114) = 5.036, p = 0.027, $\eta 2p$ = 0.044]. The interaction effect remained significant also after controlling [F (1,113) = 5.48, p = 0.021, $\eta 2p$ = 0.050].
Proximity	Across the three studies, average consumption per meeting attendee was 74 g (SD = 43) for study 1; 78 g (SD = 43) for study 2 and 87 g (SD = 35) for study 3. In the first study, manipulation of perceived variety and information leaflets did not affect intake. In the second study, significantly more vegetables were eaten when they were offered in single sized portions (M = 97 g, SD = 45) versus in a shared multiple portions bowl (63 g, SD = 38) (p < 0.001). In the third study, no effect was found of the additional availability of cookies on vegetable consumption during the meeting.
Proximity	Using the example of sustainable (more expensive) plastic water bottles, pro-environmental priming can nudge individuals towards making more sustainable choices even if it comes at a higher cost. The effects of search were similar for lab-based participants who received pro-environmental guidance. These participants also decreased their willingness to buy bottled water and switched to preferring mountain spring water and natural artesian water instead of purified drinking water. However, the effects on plastic preferences were limited to only plant-based plastic bottles. Participants who had received no guidance and who had not yet searched online, seemed to gravitate toward purified drinking water. Little attention seemed to be paid to the type of plastic used in the bottles.
Proximity	No main effects were found. A significant interaction between snack type and chocolate position was found (p = 0.010, $\eta 2$ = 0.159), with fruit consumption being significantly higher when chocolate was located at a 20 cm distance compared to 70 cm (53.35 g vs. 22.35 g, p = 0.042). Higher visual salience of each snack type correlated to more of the snack being consumed, ps < 0.017. The consumption of a snack did not depend on its position, but rather the relative position of another snack. To maximize choice of healthy items, it is advisable for supermarkets to move healthy items closer and unhealthy items further away.

Authors, Year, Journal, Country	Participants
Van Gestel, L. C. et al. 2020 Frontiers in Psychology Netherlands	N^i = 134 (85 women, an average age of 41.86, SD = 18.22) N^{ii} = 412 (353 women, an average age of 44.63, SD = 17.56) The main dependent variable was whether or not participants chose the target chocolate (which was positioned most proximally in the nudge conditions).
van Kleef, E. et al. 2020 International Journal of Environmental Research and Public Health Netherlands	A quasi-experimental study was carried out at two vocational schools (Ede, Velp) over a 10-month period. The study recorded 17 healthier choices and 263 unhealthy choices on display in Ede, and 381 healthier and 139 unhealthy choices in Velp. Of these products, the largest categories were beverages and sweet snacks in Ede (50% and 14% of the total number of products on display, respectively), and beverages and dairy in Velp (28% and 29%, respectively).
Jinghui, H. 2017 Journal of Computer-Mediated Communication United States	N^i = 91 (University administrative staff) N^{ii} = 92 (College students)

Focus area	Key Findings
Proximity	The proximity nudge was effective in stimulating the choice for a specific article regardless of the number of options in the choice set. Participants of Study 1 were more than twice as likely to choose the target chocolate when this option was positioned proximally than when it was not positioned proximally, $\chi^2 (1) = 5.42$, $p = 0.020$, $b = 0.85$ (SE = 0.37), $p = 0.021$, OR = 2.33, 95% CI [1.14, 4.87]. The study also revealed a main effect of the number of options, $b = -1.53$ (SE = 0.41), $p < 0.001$, OR = 0.22, 95% CI [0.09, 0.47], indicating that participants were about 4.5 times more likely to choose the target chocolate when offered three options than when offered nine options. Study 2 replicated the main results of Study 1 and revealed strong evidence for the effectiveness of the proximity nudge on the likelihood of choosing the target chocolate regardless the number of options involved.
Proximity	Increasing the availability of healthier products in school canteens leads to small positive changes in sales of products (particularly beverages and sandwiches). Sales of healthier products increased from 31% in the baseline period to almost 36% in the final period of the school year. About half of the displayed beverages of the canteen were healthier options with less or no sugar. This percentage was mirrored in sales (45.3% healthier in the abrupt changing canteen, 53% in the gradually changing canteen). Throughout the study period, the share of sales of healthier beverages increased from 42% to 51%. This shows that increasing the relative share of displayed healthier products can make a difference, but particularly in situations where consumers are quite indifferent in their choices between available options.
Salience	Interface cues on a food-ordering website signaling the amount of food that other users consume trigger an anchoring heuristic and induce individuals to model that amount when deciding their own consumption volume. In Study 1, individuals would order more food when the initial anchor was set at a high level than set at a low level. A Welch's t-test showed that low-anchor participants (M = 3.47, SD = 2.41) ordered significantly fewer cookies than high-anchor participants (M = 8.59, SD = 4.02), Welch = 43.83, $p < 0.001$. Study II demonstrated that participants rated other people's order quantity as significantly less important than other introspective factors in reaching their decisions on how many cookies to order: liking the food (M = 5.24, SD = 1.79; $p < 0.001$), its taste (M = 4.61, SD = 1.95; $p < 0.001$), being in the mood for that kind of food (M = 4.54, SD = 1.91; $p < 0.001$), and hunger level (M = 4.39, SD = 2.06; $p = 0.005$).

Authors, Year, Journal, Country	Participants
Ghoniem, A., van Dillen, L. F., and Hofmann, W. 2020 Appetite Germany	N^i = 102 (82 females, 20 males, Mage = 22.13 years, SDage = 5.69) Participants were recruited on campus at the University of Cologne N^{ii} = 138 (106 females, 32 males, Mage = 22.30 years, SDage = 3.63) Participants were recruited online.
Fennis, B. M. et al. 2020 Food Quality and Preference Netherlands	N^i = 95 (a mean age of 23.20 years, SD = 7.61, 41% females) Experiment 1 aimed to provide a first test of the hypothesis that actively associating a scarcity cue with a healthy food would boost consumption, particularly among consumers with a fast, rather than slow life history strategy. This study featured actual consumption of a healthy food item (green grapes) as its main dependent variable. N^{ii} = 233 (Mage = 30.10, SDage = 9.43, 58.8% females) The main dependent variable in Experiment 2 was the intention to buy a healthy food item (dried cranberries).
Thunström, L. 2018 Journal Of Economic Behavior and Organization United States	N = 341 (out of total 410) (The general student and staff population at the University of Wyoming). Participants were physically endowed with an eight-ounce jar of honey of unknown origin. They were then given the option to pay to switch their endowed jar for an eight-ounce jar of locally produced Wyoming honey.

Focus area	Key Findings
Salience	Food desire peaks when the availability of tempting food stimuli is accompanied by high need states and a positive learning experience. With Experiment 1, a simple t-test on desire by experimental condition revealed a main effect of availability, such that desire was more pronounced in the presence of the candy, MEG = 2.62, SDEG = 1.84, as compared to its absence, MCG = 1.42, SDCG = 1.43; t (100) = 3.67, p < 0.001, d = 0.73. With Experiment 2, a simple t-test on desire by experimental condition revealed a main effect of availability, such that desire was more pronounced in the presence, MEG = 0.83, SDEG = 0.76, as compared to absence, MCG = 0.51, SDCG = 0.61 of the food stimuli, t(136) = 2.69, p = 0.008, d = 0.46. Hence, the main effect for stimulus availability from Experiment 1 was replicated.
Salience	Consumers with a fast life-history strategy are more susceptible to scarcity cues to foster healthy choice. For slow life-history strategy consumers, it is abundance cues. Acute food craving mediates the impact of cue type for fast strategists. Socially validated trust fulfills this role for slow strategists. While the main effect of LHS was non-significant (B = -0.37, SE = 0.68, t < 1.), exposure to scarcity cues significantly increased actual consumption of grapes compared to the control condition (B = 4.78, SE = 0.79, t(91) = 6.05, p = 0.0001). Importantly, the interaction between type of cue (scarcity vs. control) and LHS proved to be significant and qualified the main effect (B = -3.28, SE = 1.36, t(91) = -2.41, p = 0.02, r = 0.21). The main effect of cue types (scarcity vs. abundance) on the intention to buy the healthy food item was not significant (B = 0.06, SE = 0.22, t < 1), nor was the main effect of LHS (B = 0.06, SE = 0.06, t < 1). However, the interaction between type of appeal and LHS was highly significant (B = -0.37, SE = 0.11, t (2 2 9) = -3.26, p = 0.001, r = 0.21).
Salience	Both "opportunity cost reminders" (i.e., nudges that increase the salience of costs to spending today) and "spending booster reminders focusing on the benefits of buying local" increased discomfort of paying with lower bid amounts for tightwads (at the 1% level) while not affecting spending by the other consumer types (spendthrifts and unconflicted consumers). Wilcoxon Mann-Whitney and t-tests of equality of the spending levels imply (i) none of the nudges impacts average spending, (ii) tightwads spend less than unconflicted: both the Wilcoxon Mann-Whitney test, p-value = 0.027, and a one-sided t-test, p-value = 0.005, reject the null hypothesis that spending by unconflicted, and tightwads is the same, (iii) tightwads reduce their spending as a result of both nudges compared to when not being nudged. Both a Wilcoxon Mann-Whitney test (p-value = 0.064) and a two-sided t-test (p-value = 0.034) reject the null hypothesis that tightwad

Authors, Year, Journal, Country	Participants
Thunström, L. *(continue)*	
Ozturk, O. D. et al. 2020 Journal of Economic Behavior and Organization United States	N = 48 000 observations The study was conducted in 18 elementary schools divided into nine pairs based on the percentage of students receiving free or reduced-price lunches. Data for 26 school days before treatment were collected. There was then a 9-week treatment period. During this period, modified menus and promotional items were used in the treated schools.
Venema, T. et al. 2020 Appetite Netherlands	N=123 (Recruited on campus, mean age 21.42, SD = 4.09, 61.5% women) The aim of the study was to investigate whether a portion size nudge has the potential to work in accordance with (instead of against) existing habits. It was tested whether a portion size nudge would be more effective in reducing the amount of sugar added to tea when people have a strong habit of adding a fixed number of teaspoons of sugar to a cup of tea. The study had a mixed factorial design with teaspoon size (reduced size vs. control) as a within-subject factor, and habit disruption context condition (hot tea vs. cold tea) as a between-subjects factor.
Kosīte, D. et al. 2019 International Journal of Behavioral Nutrition and Physical Activity United Kingdom	N = 134 (Ages 18–61) The sample was randomly allocated to one of two groups varying in the size of plate used for self-serving lunch: large or small. The primary outcome was amount of food energy (kcal) consumed during a meal.
Coucke, N. et al. 2019 Foods Not mentioned. Conducted in the butcher counter of a local supermarket of a mid-sized European city	The study hypothesizes that increasing (decreasing) the display area size and quantity of displayed raw meat products within this display area will lead to more (fewer) sales of these meat products.

Focus area	Key Findings
	spending is the same over no nudge and the opportunity cost reminder nudge. Further, the null hypothesis that tightwad spending is the same over no nudge and the spending booster nudge is weakly rejected (Wilcoxon Mann-Whitney test, p-value = 0.139; one-sided t-test, p-value = 0.069).
Size nudges	During the treatment period, selection of the healthy entrées increased on average by about 15%. This change was not due to the changes in composition of the school lunch crowd, i.e., the treatment did not differentially affect school lunch participation. Though the treatment effect at the first incidence of the nudge was twice the size of the average treatment effects in models without this distinction; subsequent nudges failed to differentially change the selection of a given healthy entrée. There was also no evidence of habit formation when selection rates for healthy entrées were compared pre-, during and post-treatment periods. Differential change in post treatment was a statistical zero.
Size nudges	People who have a strong habit to add a fixed number of teaspoons of sugar to their tea would be more susceptible to the effect of the portion size nudge. There was a significant effect of spoon size on sugar usage, t (123) = -6.17, p < 0.001, Cohen's d = 0.56. Participants used significantly more sugar with the normal sized spoon (Mgrams = 5.13, SD = 4.81) than with the smaller spoon, Mgrams = 3.50, SD = 2.64. Changing the normal sized teaspoon for a smaller teaspoon reduced participants' sugar usage by approximately 27% (SD = 32.92).
Size nudges	There was no clear evidence of a difference in consumption between the two groups: Cohen's d = 0.07 (95% CI [-0.27, 0.41]), with participants in the large plate group consuming on average 19.2 (95% CI [-76.5, 115.0]) more calories (3%) compared to the small plate group (large: mean (SD) = 644.1 (265.0) kcal, versus small: 624.9 (292.3) kcal). The difference between the groups was not modified by individual characteristics. There was no evidence of impact on meal micro-structure, with the exception of more food being left on the plate when larger plates were used.
Size nudges	Changing the size of the display area and the number of products displayed created a shift in the consumers' purchase behavior of meat. There was a significant effect of the store type on the weight sold (F (1, 17,448) = 48.94, p < 0.001). Sales in the experimental store (mean (M) = 0.85, standard deviation (SD) = 2.17) were significantly lower than these in the control store (M = 1.1,

Authors, Year, Journal, Country	Participants
Coucke, N. et al. *(continue)*	The size of the display area and quantity of displayed poultry products, serving as the nudging intervention, were increased at the expanse of less sustainable meat products.
Garnett, E. E. et al. 2019 Proceedings of the National Academy of Sciences of the United States of America United Kingdom	N = 94,644 (Meals purchased in 2017 in three cafeterias at an English university)
Petit, O. et al. 2018 Marketing Letters France	N^i = 102 (46 females, mean age = 30.65 years, SD = 9.38, recruited online) N^{ii} = 76 Undergraduate students (22 females, mean age = 21, SD = 3.04) took part in the study for extra credit. The study ran as a two-condition (portion illusion: larger vs. smaller) between-participant experimental design. The study hypothesized that: H1: People will express greater purchase intentions when the food pictured on the front of the packaging is displayed on a smaller (larger) portion illusion rather than on a larger plate (smaller portion illusion). H2: People will evaluate a food product as more appetizing when the food pictured on the front of the packaging is displayed on a smaller rather than on a larger plate. H3: The number of mental simulations of the eating experience will moderate the impact of the Delboeuf illusion on the amount of food served. H4: People will select less food to eat when the food pictured on the front of the packaging is displayed on a smaller rather than on a larger plate.

Focus area	Key Findings
	SD = 2.56). There was also a significant effect of the meat type on the weight sold (F (2, 17,448) = 641.83, p < 0.001). Sales of poultry (M = 1.91, SD = 3.67) were significantly higher (p < 0.001) than those of other meat products (M = 0.65, SD = 1.49) and significantly higher (p < 0.001) than the sales of pork (M = 0.41, SD = 0.84). There was no significant effect of timing on the weight sold (F (2, 17,448) = 1.25, p = 0.287). Thus, the average weight sold of all meat products together was similar before, during and after the intervention period (Before: M = 0.96, SD = 2.36; During: M = 1.02; SD = 2.54; After: M = 0.95, SD = 2.21).
Size nudges	Doubling the proportion of vegetarian meals available from 25 to 50% (e.g., from 1in2 to 2in4 options) increased vegetarian meal sales by 14.9 and 14.5% in the observational study (Two cafeterias) and by 7.8% in the experimental study (one cafeteria), equivalent to proportional increases in vegetarian meal sales of 61.8%, 78.8%, and 40.8% respectively.
Size nudges	Presenting a portion of food in a smaller (vs. larger) plate or bowl creates the illusion of a larger (vs. smaller) portion, although the quantity of food remains the same (the Delboeuf illusion). This nudged consumers to find food more desirable, while at the same time reducing their consumption. Experiment 1: A Mann-Whitney test indicated that the pizza was rated as looking significantly larger (by 20.18%) when shown on the smaller plate (M=3.94, SD=1.43) than on the larger plate (M=3.32, SD=1.54, U=988, p=0.03, r=-0.21). Confirming Hypothesis 1, participants expressed higher purchase intentions when the pizza was displayed on the smaller plate (M=4.6, SD=1.81) than on the larger plate (M=3.80, SD=.1.82, U= 985, p= 0.03, r=-0.23. Confirming Hypothesis 4, the participants in experiment 1 selected a smaller percentage of the pizza (-19.09%) on the smaller (M=33.69%, SD=16.34) than in the larger plate condition (M=41.64%, SD=19.46, t (100)=2.24, p=0.03; Cohen's d=0.44. Controlling for the portion size illusion, the self-reported number of mental simulations did not significantly affect the percentage of pizza selected (p=0.11). Thus, Hypothesis 3 was not confirmed. Experiment 2: The caloric content of the smaller-rimmed bowl (M=179.87 cal, SD=82.15) was rated as significantly higher (26.86%) than that of the larger-rimmed bowl (M=141.79 cal, SD=73.55, U=511.50, p=0.03, r=-0.25). Confirming Hypothesis 2, participants evaluated the cereals as looking more appetizing when shown in the smaller-rimmed bowl (M=3.45, SD=1.33) than in the larger-rimmed bowl (M=2.76, SD=1.48, U= 511.50, p= 0.03, r=-0.26). In support of Hypotheses 3, the vividness of mental simulations moderated the effect of the portion size illusion on the food serving (β=11.44, t(72)=2.61, p=0.01). Examination of the interaction plot revealed that those participants with

Authors, Year, Journal, Country	Participants
Petit, O. et al. *(continue)*	
Labbe, D. et al. 2018 Nutrients Switzerland	N^i = 70 (Women, ages 35–55) N^{ii} = 62 (Children) It was hypothesized: (1) adults selected a smaller ideal portion size for an elongated product than for wider and thicker shapes, (2) children's perception of food quantity was primarily driven by number of pieces, with smaller effects of size and elongation.
Vermote, M. et al. 2018 Nutrition Journal Belgium	N^i = 2056 N^{ii} = 2175 (French fries' consumption and plate waste were measured in 2056 consumers at baseline and 2175 consumers at intervention in the on-campus restaurant. French fries' portions were reduced by 20% by replacing the usual porcelain bowl served during the baseline week (±200 g) with smaller volume paper bags during the intervention week (±159 g) in a pre-post real-life experiment.
Villinger, K. et al. 2021 BMC Nutrition Germany	N = 17,233 (hot beverages sold over the course of four weeks) Sugar shakers in a university take-away café were functionally modified to reduce the amount of

Focus area	Key Findings
	medium and high scores of mental simulations poured less cereals (-23.16%, -36.23%, respectively) after seeing the smaller-rimmed bowl (MMedium mental simulations=41.12 g, MHigh mental simulations=41.96) than after seeing the larger-rimmed bowl (MMedium mental simulations=53.51 g, CI=3.78, 21.01, MHigh mental simulations=65.80, CI=11.70, 35.98). Those participants with low mental simulation scores did not change their serving behavior as a function of the portion size illusion (MLarger portion illusion=40.27 g, MSmaller portion illusion=41.23, CI=-11.46, 13.36. Confirming Hypothesis 4, participants poured less cereals (-19.72%) from the packaging showing the smaller-rimmed bowl (M=41.26 g, SD=14.91) than from the packaging showing the larger-rimmed bowl (M=51.39 g, SD=24.80, t(74)=2.16, p=0.03, Cohen's d=0.50).
Size nudges	Adults selected a smaller portion size for an elongated product than for wider and thicker shapes. Ideal self-selected portion size for ice cream was significantly impacted by shape ($F(5,345) = 11.8$, $p < 0.001$). The smallest selected portion size was observed with the elongated shape, TALLER (mean = 94.8 mL, SD = 21.8), which was significantly smaller than the portion size obtained with the WIDER (mean = 100.1 mL, SD = 20.4) and THICKER variants (mean = 105.6 mL, SD = 21.4). Children's perception of food quantity was primarily driven by number of pieces, with smaller effects of size and elongation. The number of presented pieces had a significant effect on the number selected ($F (3,1464) = 1302.1$; $p < 0.01$, $\eta 2p = 0.72$). Overall, children selected a number of reference gummy candies close to the number presented in the test pile. Perceived quantity was not influenced by color variety. These findings suggest that it may be possible to reduce the size of food portions without negatively impacting perceived quantity, and to provide opportunities to nudge consumers towards smaller portions while maintaining satisfaction.
Size nudges	The total intake of French fries decreased by 9.1% when replacing the usual porcelain bowl with smaller volume paper bags.
Priming	Modifying the functional design of sugar shakers resulted in a reduction of added sugar by 20% (d = 1.35) compared to the default condition. A total of 59 customers evaluated the intervention at the end of the study. They regarded the intervention as a helpful

Authors, Year, Journal, Country	Participants
Villinger, K. et al. *(continue)*	sugar in each pour by 47%. In addition, 59 customers (62% female; 78% students) with a mean age of M = 26 years (SD = 7.3) and an average BMI of M = 22.4 kg/m² (SD = 3.6) were surveyed to evaluate the acceptance of the intervention.
Robinson, E. and Kersbergen, I. 2018 American Journal of Clinical Nutrition United Kingdom	N = 40 (Staff and students at the University of Liverpool.) Across 3 experiments, participants were served a larger or a smaller portion of food. In experiments 1 and 2, participants selected and consumed a portion of that food 24 hours later. In experiment 3, participants reported on their preferred ideal portion size of that food after 1 week.
Vandenbroele, J. et al. 2018 Food Quality and Preference Belgium	N = 161 (59% female) A field experiment with meat sausage as focal product, was conducted over a month in a branch of a large European retailer, generating shopping receipts.
Hawkins, L. et al. 2021 Appetite United Kingdom	N = 169 Female students (Mean age = 20.9; mean BMI = 23.3) were assigned to either a high energy-dense snack (HED), low energy-dense (LED) snack foods or control condition, where they viewed 3 types of images (HED foods, LED foods and interior design as control), Participants completed questionnaires were provided a snack buffet of grapes and cookies.
Morren, M. et al. 2021 Journal of Environmental Psychology Netherlands	N^i = 1264 N^{ii} = 737

Focus area	Key Findings
	(M = 5.56, SD = 0.99), effective (M = 5.39, SD = 1.27), and adequate (M = 5.29, SD = 1.22) strategy for reducing sugar consumption.
Size nudges	Reducing food portion sizes may decrease how much consumers choose to eat. The consumption of a smaller, as opposed to a larger, portion size of a food resulted in participants believing a "normal"-sized portion was smaller (experiments 1–3, $p \leq 0.001$), consuming less of that food 1 day later (experiments 1–2, $p \leq 0.003$), and displaying a tendency toward choosing a smaller ideal portion of that food 1 week later (experiment 3, $p = 0.07$), although the latter finding was not significant.
Size nudges	Adding smaller portions to a default choice architecture can nudge consumers towards buying smaller sized items. 52% of the units sold were smaller portions (small or medium), such that 100% proportion of default portion size units sold in the preceding month was significantly higher than the proportion default units sold during the intervention (48%), $z = 10.3$, $p < 0.001$). While assuming an equal number of units sold regardless of the setting, we note that 13% less meat (in kg) would have been sold, due to the purchases of smaller portions. The researchers observed a significant effect of the portion size choice (100g, 125g, or 150g) on the total amount bought in a kg, F $(2,158) = 6.83$, $p = 0.001$. The total amount of sausage bought by customers purchasing the medium portion size (n = 50, M = 0.37, SD = 1.63) also was statistically lower than the amount bought by default portion size buyers, $p = 0.046$. However, no significant differences were found between the small and medium portion buyers, $p = 0.57$.
Social norms	Although the three types of socially endorsed images did not significantly affect participants' individual consumption of grapes and cookies, viewing socially endorsed images of LED foods (versus HED foods) led to participants consuming a higher proportion of grapes compared to cookies (F(2) = 3.22, p = 0.04, partial eta squared = 0.04).
Social norms	Procedural information about health had most potential to influence dietary behavior.

Authors, Year, Journal, Country	Participants
Griesoph, A. et al. 2021 Sustainability Germany	N = 13,907 (2 university canteens)
Gonçalves, D. et al. 2021 Sustainability Portugal	N = 1636 (Supermarket customers)
Ewert, B. 2017 Social Theory & Health Germany	N = 0
Huitink, M. et al. 2020 Appetite Netherlands	N = 244 (Supermarket customers, 123 on the intervention days) The effect of a combination of 2 nudging strategies in shopping trolleys was investigated: a social norm about vegetable purchases and a designated place to put vegetables; on the quantity of vegetables purchased in a supermarket.

Focus area	Key Findings
Social norms Before entering the canteen, the participants filled in the questionnaire, then they bought their lunch. Behind the cash desks, there were placed two ballot boxes, one for the questionnaire of the participants who had chosen a vegan/vegetarian dish and one for the questionnaires of those who had chosen a dish with meat or fish.	The study detected significant effects for the control variables age (β = -0.020, p = 0.039, odds ratio = 0.980) and gender (β = 1.011, p = 0.000, odds ratio = 2.750) indicating that younger and female participants are more likely to choose a vegan/vegetarian meal. The study shows a remarkable nudging effect of guessed norms: The higher the presumed proportion of vegetarian dishes sold, the lower the probability of choosing a vegetarian dish.
Social norms The study sought whether a message conveying fruit and vegetable purchasing norms positioned in strategic places might effectively change food choices. The purchase quantities were measured over 3 months and compared with the corresponding period of the previous year.	The study showed overall average increases of 30% in the variety of fruits and vegetables purchased, and overall average increases of 25% in the quantity of fruits and vegetables purchased, t (2955) = 14.176, p = 0.000.
Social norms	Nudges have three drawbacks in comparison to setting-based health promotion. Firstly, they exclusively promote students' behavioral prevention while disregarding measures of structural prevention. Secondly, choice architects are likely to enforce cultural homogeneity when defining the meaning of school health, i.e., the right food or dose of exercise, while deviating lifestyles are implicitly judged to be irrational and unhealthy. Thirdly, within a nudge-based approach students are predominantly addressed as consumers (nudges), while less attention is paid to other social identities such as citizens or co-producers.
Social norms	A nudge inlay in shopping trolleys communicating a social norm of vegetable purchases and indicating a distinct place to put vegetables in the trolley increased purchases of vegetables. The customers on the intervention days (n = 123) were in a higher tertile for grams of vegetables purchased compared to the customers on the control days (OR: 1.66, 95% CI: 1.03–2.69, p = 0.03), especially those who bought groceries for less than three days (OR: 3.24, 95% CI: 1.43–7.35, p = 0.003). Sensitivity analyses also showed that intervention customers who noticed the green inlay were even more likely to purchase more vegetables (OR: 1.86, 95% CI: 1.06–3.25, p = 0.02).

Authors, Year, Journal, Country	Participants
Otto, A. S. et al. 2019 Journal of Consumer Affairs United States	Provincial norms reduce the total calories purchased at a Cinnabon retail outlet in New York City N^i = 166 (50% Female; Mage = 39.82) (Cinnabon customers, 50% female; Mage = 39.82) N^{ii} = 60 Undergraduate participants (70% male; Mage = 20.23) were randomly assigned to one of three conditions: a provincial norm condition, a descriptive norm condition, or a control condition. For this experiment, a numeric norm similar to a one-cup serving of other types of desserts was selected (e.g., ice cream, chocolate mousse, pudding, chocolate cake, or brownie) ranging from 250 to 400 cal and equaling to a MiniBon roll (350 cal). N^{iii} = 150 Undergraduate participants (59% male; Mage = 20.45) were randomly assigned to one of three conditions: a provincial norm condition, a descriptive norm condition, or a control condition. They participated in a study on restaurant menus. It was hypothesized that provincial norms reduce the total calories purchased at a Cinnabon retail outlet in New York City.
Hogreve, J. et al. 2020 Journal of Retailing Germany	N^i = 89 Parents (69.6% female), Mean Age (Parents) = 37.36 (SD = 6.1), Mean Age (Children) = 5.9 (SD = 2.46) dining at a fast-food restaurant with at least one child. N^{ii} =164 Parents (79% female, Mean Aage (Parents) = 36 (SD = 8.28), Mean Age (Children) = 6.1 (SD = 2.66) N^{ii} = 155 Parents (68% female, Mean Age (Parents) = 37 (SD = 5.99), Mean Age (Children) = 5.9 (SD = 3.06) N^{iii} = 288 Parents (70.8% female, Mage (Parents) = 38 (SD = 6.36), Mean Age(Children) = 6.4 (2.71)

Focus area	Key Findings
Social norms	Exposure to low-calorie provincial norms prompted consumers to make healthier consumption decisions. The analysis revealed a significant effect of condition on the number of calories purchased, $F_{(2,163)} = 5.27$, $p = 0.006$. The provincial norm reduced calories purchased relative to the control ($p = 0.037$) and descriptive norm ($p = 0.008$) conditions, with no difference between the descriptive norm and control conditions ($p > 0.88$).
	In Experiment 2, results revealed a significant effect of condition on the number of calories ordered, $F_{(2,57)} = 4.95$, $p = 0.010$. Consistent with Experiment1, the provincial norm significantly decreased the total calories ordered relative to the control ($p = 0.004$) and descriptive norm ($p = 0.024$) conditions. The descriptive norm did not influence the total calories ordered relative to the control ($p > 0.50$). The provincial norm reduced calories purchased relative to the control ($p = 0.037$) and descriptive norm ($p = 0.008$) conditions with no difference between the descriptive norm and control conditions ($p > 0.88$).
	In Experiment 3, results revealed a significant effect of condition on the total number of topping calories ordered, $F_{(2,147)} = 5.05$, $p = 0.008$. The provincial norm condition significantly decreased the total topping calories ordered relative to the control ($p = 0.002$) and the descriptive norm ($p = 0.032$) conditions. The descriptive norm condition did not differ from the control ($p > 0.35$).
	Analysis of the total calories ordered (i.e., topping calories + cup size calories) again revealed a significant effect of condition, $F_{(2,147)} = 3.97$, $p = 0.021$. Those in the provincial norm condition ordered significantly fewer calories overall relative to those in the control ($p = 0.01$) and descriptive norm ($p = 0.028$) conditions. The descriptive norm condition did not alter the total calories ordered relative to the control ($p > 0.69$).
Social norms	Parents with a high tendency to engage in social comparison and a malleable view of the self are most likely to conform to the norm towards making healthier choices in their parental social network. In Study 1, parents' scores on the social comparison orientation scale significantly affected their choice of healthy/less healthy side items ($\beta = -0.45$, Wald $\chi^2 (1) = 4.42$, $p = 0.036$), in a way that parents with a higher social comparison orientation were less likely to choose a healthy side item for their children.
	In Study 2, results revealed a marginally significant negative effect of social comparison orientation ($\beta = -0.23$, $Z = -1.68$, $p = 0.09$), such that those with a higher social comparison orientation were less likely to choose healthy side items. We did not find a significant main effect of implicit theories of the self ($\beta = -0.19$, $Z = -1.64$, $p > 0.1$). Most importantly, however, the results revealed a significant interaction ($\beta = -0.18$, $Z = -1.99$, $p = 0.046$) between social orientation and implicit self-theories, as predicted in H2.

Authors, Year, Journal, Country	Participants
Hogreve, J. et al. *(continue)*	It was hypothesized that: H1: Parents with a high social comparison orientation are more likely to conform to the food choices of other parents in their social networks for their own children compared to parents with a low social comparison orientation. H2: Social comparison orientation and self-theories interact to influence the extent to which parents conform to the food choices of other parents in their social networks. Parents with a high social comparison orientation and a malleable theory of the self will conform to a greater extent than any other parental group. H3: Presence (vs. absence) of a descriptive social norm of choosing healthy food for children significantly increases choice of healthy foods for children among the individuals most sensitive to information about what other parents in their social network are choosing (i.e., parents with a high social comparison orientation and a malleable theory of the self). Presence or absence of a descriptive social norm will not affect choices made by parents with a different combination of social comparison orientation and self-theory.

Source: Authors

We believe that our analysis provides a comprehensive overview of the studies we analyzed. We see the benefit of our analysis in the fact that we not only provide an overview of the existing literature, but that in doing so we reduce the high cost of finding, sorting, and analyzing the available resources relating to food nudges for future researchers. The results in the foregoing table can be used as a resource for increasing the scope of the secondary literature on the topic.

Focus area	Key Findings
	Participants exposed to the fixed theory prime (MFixed = 3.61) differed significantly from those exposed to the malleable theory prime (MMalleable = 4.35; $F(1, 155)$ = 9.36, $p < 0.05$) on the implicit theories measure ($\alpha = 0.89$, M = 3.97). The study found a main effect of social comparison orientation, replicating support for H1 (b = -0.47, Z = -3.23, $p < 0.01$), such that parents with a high social comparison orientation were less likely to order healthy side items. As in Study 2a, a main effect of implicit self-theories (b = -0.19, Z = -1.06, $p > 0.1$) was found. Instead, a significant interaction between scores on the social comparison orientation scale and manipulated self-theory (fixed or malleable) was revealed (b = -0.31, Z = -2.13, $p = 0.033$), as predicted in H2. In Study 3, a total of 39.4% of the respondents chose at least one option perceived as healthy when they did not receive healthy norm information, compared to 51.0% of those who received the healthy social norm treatment (b = 0.27, Z = 4.53, $p = 0.03$), consistent with past research showing the power of social norms to influence behavior. This represents an increase of over 29% in the percentage of parents choosing at least one healthy side item as part of the children's meal because of the social norm intervention. Most importantly, as hypothesized in H3, the results reveal a significant 3-way interaction (b = 0.138, Z = 4.00, $p = 0.045$).

Conclusion

The study of nudges and nudging is a relatively new field its core being the many factors that influence human behavior. A nudge is successful when it influences an individual to voluntarily (i.e., without coercion) change their behavior, resulting in the nudge benefiting both the individual and society as a whole. Our analysis of nudging was focused on health issues (primarily bariatrics and diabetology).

We identified three questions that our research should answer. We focused our first research question on a comparative analysis of the epistemological foundations of the study of human behavior, especially with regard to the theory of *Homo economicus* and prospect theory. We showed that the model of rational human behavior based on the axiom that human beings are *Homo economicus* is in turn based on Cartesian rationalism and epistemology, and the assumption that actors have perfect information. In reality, however, the assumption of human rationality is problematic because a completely rational reaction to an event requires full knowledge of all relevant facts, which is rarely possible. Rational thinking would be easy if we knew all the conditions relevant to our initial premises. In reality, however, that is impossible. Herbert Simon responded to this problem with his concept of "bounded rationality." Simon recognized that Cartesian rationalism cannot fully explain and predict human actions and their consequences. Subsequent experiments by Preston and Baratta with the behavior of people at auctions found an anomaly that could not be explained by models built on the assumption that humans are *Homo economicus*. A new paradigm was born, which was later developed into prospect theory by Kahneman and Tversky. We consider prospect theory to be a reaction to a "Kuhn anomaly" in experimental results. The Kuhn anomaly in this case signaled that the explanatory power of the idea of *Homo economicus* was falling apart. Of course, models built on the axiom of *Homo economicus* did not necessarily cease to be valid in their entirety.

The thing changing is the researchers' confidence in the conclusions arising from their models. Absolute statements of scientific certainty have been replaced by relativistic statements. In that process, absolute predictions do not persist. Classical (Cartesian) rationalism has disintegrated, and a new epistemology was born, that is, creating a new picture of the world and a new explanatory and interpretive paradigm. In economics, this new paradigm is known as behavioral economics, which includes prospect theory. We have a new phenomenon: the nudge.

Our second research question was in essence, how do classical theory and prospect theory differ? We concluded that the explanatory paradigms behind classical economic currents of thought and the ones behind prospect theory differ significantly, both methodologically and epistemologically. Prospect theory questions the absolute validity of the classical theory postulates of rational choices made by human beings who are, in effect, *Homo economicus*. It turns out that human behavior is influenced by a number of other, non-rational factors.

We reviewed the literature and the detailed research it provided to find an answer to the third research question: What are the policy tools available for performing food nudges? We searched the literature for any discussion of factors that have the nature of a nudge in the field of nutrition and diabetology. We identified the following types of nudges: (a) priming and labeling, (b) positioning, proximity, and size effects, (c) the decoy effect, (d) presentation of a default, baseline option, (e) monetary incentives, (f) framing, (g) significance effect, (h) social norms, and (i) combinations of one or more of those nudges. We examined the nudges in detail on the basis of our search of the scientific literature in the area of food nudges. Our analysis provides an idea of the frequency with which particular kinds of nudges appear in the scientific discourse. We also provide important information about the different types of nudges and suggestions for how to use them to create a system for encouraging health and healthy eating habits. Our review of the literature revealed that the study of food nudges in individual countries had developed very unevenly across the world.

Summary

The book deals with the problem of nudge and nudging. Its core is the study of factors influencing human behavior. The nudge characteristically influences human behavior resulting in a change that is voluntary (without external coercion) and benefits the individual society as a whole. The book focuses on finding answers to three research questions. The first research question is aimed at a comparative analysis of the epistemological foundations of human behavior in a model based on the *Homo economicus* axiom and in the prospect theory. We show that human behavior depicted in a rational model constructed on the axiom of *Homo economicus* is based on Cartesian rationalism and Cartesian epistemology as well as the assumption of perfect information. However, in reality this type of rationality is problematic because complete rationality of action requires complete knowledge of all the relevant facts. This is, in reality, impossible. Anomalies are emerging and the models built on the *Homo economicus* axiom cannot sufficiently explain them. H. Simon responds to this problem with the concept of bounded rationality, where man's actions and their consequences cannot be fully explained and predicted using Cartesian rationalism. Subsequent Preston and Baratta's experiments with the behavior of people at auctions point to an anomaly that cannot be explained by models built on the assumption of the *Homo economicus* axiom. a new paradigm is born, later developed as a prospect theory (Kahneman and Tversky). We consider prospect theory as an example of a reaction to the Kuhn anomaly in a scientific explanation. This anomaly signals that the originally absolute belief in the idea of *Homo economicus* is falling apart. Classical (Cartesian) rationalism loses its original supposed absolute validity. A neo-nationalist epistemology is born with a new scientific picture of the world and a new explanatory and interpretive paradigm. In economics, this is known as behavioral economics. The explanatory paradigm in classical economic stream and in prospect theory differs significantly, both methodologically and epistemologically. Prospect theory questions the absolute validity of the postulates of the theory of (classical) rational choice based on the axiom of *Homo economicus*. It turns out that human behavior is influenced by a number of other factors that are non-rational in nature. Based on a content analysis of the literature and a systematic review, factors that have the nature of nudge in the area of nudging for a healthy diet are sought. The following factors were identified: (a) priming and labeling, (b) positioning, proximity, and size effects, (c) decoy effect, (d) defaults, (e) monetary incentives, (f) framing, (g) salience effect, (h) social norms, (i) combinations of these factors. A systematic review of the literature has revealed that the issue is developer significantly uneven as far as individual countries are concerned. The countries of Central Europe (including the Czech Republic) are, unlike the USA and the countries of Western Europe, at the very beginning of nudge research. An analysis of the literature at the same time shows that there is a high rate of obesity in countries where research on health and eating habits lags behind the world. And this is a risk factor for many diseases. The identified factors of nudging for a healthy diet and the methodological way of their use can become an incentive for public policy actors to set up a system employing behavioral approaches for a healthy diet.

References

Ackermann, R. (2019). Effect on Health Care Expenditures During Nationwide Implementation of the Diabetes Prevention Program as a Health Insurance Benefit. *Diabetes Care* 42 (9): 1776-83. doi:10.2337/dc18-2071.

Acton, R. and Hammond, D. (2018). The Impact of Price and Nutrition Labelling on Sugary Drink Purchases: Results from an Experimental Marketplace Study. *Appetite* 121:129-37. doi:10.1016/j.appet.2017.11.089.

Ali, M. K. et al. (2018). Advancing Health Policy and Program Research in Diabetes: Findings from the Natural Experiments for Translation in Diabetes (NEXT-D) Network. *Current Diabetes Reports* 18 (12): 146. doi:10.1007/s11892-018-1112-3.

Allan, J. L., and Powell, D. J. (2020). Prompting Consumers to Make Healthier Food Choices in Hospitals: A Cluster Randomised Controlled Trial. *Int J Behav Nutr Phys Act* 17 (1): 86. doi:10.1186/s12966-020-00990-z.

American Diabetes Association (2013). *Diagnosis and Classification of Diabetes Mellitus.* Diabetes Care 36 (1): 67-74. doi:10.2337/dc13-S067.

Amlung, M. and Mackillop, J. (2019). Availability of Legalized Cannabis Reduces Demand for Illegal Cannabis Among Canadian Cannabis Users: Evidence from a Behavioural Economic Substitution Paradigm. *Canadian Journal of Public Health* 110 (2): 216-21. doi:10.17269/s41997-018-0160-4.

Anzman-Frasca, S., Braun Abbey C., Ehrenberg, S., Epstein Leonard H. et al. (2018). Effects of a Randomized Intervention Promoting Healthy Children's Meals on Children's Ordering and Dietary Intake in a Quick-service Restaurant. *Physiology & Behavior* 192:109-17. doi:10.1016/j.physbeh.2018.01.022.

Singh, I. and Singh, S. (2021). The Hype Machine: How Social Media Disrupts Our Elections, Our Economy and Our Health – and How We Must Adapt. *Bus Soc Rev* 126 (1): 101–4. doi:10.1111/basr.12225.

Ariely, D. (2010). *Predictably Irrational: The Hidden Forces that Shape our Decisions.* New York: Harper Perennial.

Ariely, D. and Loewenstein, G. (2006). The Heat of the Moment: The Effect of Sexual Arousal on Sexual Decision Making. *Journal of Behavioral Decision Making* 19 (2): 87-98. doi:10.1002/bdm.501.

Arno, A. and Thomas, S. (2016). The Efficacy of Nudge Theory Strategies in Influencing Adult Dietary Behaviour: A Systematic Review and Meta-analysis. *BMC Public Health* 16:676. doi:10.1186/s12889-016-3272-x.

Askelson, N., Brady, P., Ryan, G., Meier, C., Ortiz, C., Scheidel, C., and Delger, P. (2018). Actively Involving Middle School Students in the Implementation of a Pilot of a Behavioral Economics – Based Lunchroom Intervention in Rural Schools. *Health Promotion Practice* 20 (5): 675-83. doi:10.1177/1524839918807717.

Attwood, S., Chesworth, S. J., and Parkin, B. L. (2020). Menu Engineering to Encourage Sustainable Food Choices When Dining Out: An Online Trial of Priced-Based Decoys. *Appetite* 149:104601. doi:10.1016/j.appet.2020.104601.

Bacon, L. and Krpan, D. (2018). (Not) Eating for the Environment: The Impact of Restaurant Menu Design on Vegetarian Food Choice. *Appetite* 125:190-200. doi:10.1016/j.appet.2018.02.006.

Bachelard, G. (1999). *Le nouvel esprit scientifique*. Paris: Presse Universitaires de France.

Baláž, V. (2014). *Komplexné volby*. Bratislava: Veda.

Baláž, V. (2009). *Riziko a neistota. Úvod do behaviorálnej ekonómie a financií*. Bratislava: Veda.

Banerjee, T., Chattaraman, V., Zou, H. et al. (2020). A Neurobehavioral Study on the Efficacy of Price Interventions in Promoting Healthy Food Choices among Low Socioeconomic Families. *Sci Rep* 10 (1): 15435. doi:10.1038/s41598-020-71082-y.

Banerjee, V. A. (1992). A Simple Model of Herd Behavior. *The Quarterly Journal of Economics* 107 (3): 797–817. doi:10.2307/2118364.

Bardach, E. A. (2000). *Practical Guide for Policy Analysis*. 2nd ed., 2–46. New York: Chatham House.

Bauer, J. M., Bietz, S., Rauber, J., and Reisch, L. A. (2021). Nudging Healthier Food Choices in a Cafeteria Setting: A Sequential Multi-Intervention Field Study. *Appetite* 160: 105106. doi:10.1016/j.appet.2021.105106.

Becker, Gary S. (1978*). The Economic Approach to Human Behavior*. Chicago: University of Chicago Press.

Belli, H. M., Chokshi, S. K. Hegde, R. et al. (2020). Implementation of a Behavioral Economics Electronic Health Record (BE-EHR) Module to Reduce Overtreatment of Diabetes in Older Adults. *J Gen Intern Med* 35 (11): 3254–61. doi:10.1007/s11606-020-06119-z.

Belsky, G. and Gilovich, T. (2000). *Why Smart People Make Big Money Mistakes and How to Correct Them: Lessons from the Life-Changing Science of Behavioral Economics*. New York: Simon & Schuster.

Benito-Ostolaza, J. M., Echavarri, R., Garcia-Prado, A., and Oses-Eraso, N. (2021). Using Visual Stimuli to Promote Healthy Snack Choices Among Children. *Social Science & Medicine* 270: 113587. doi:10.1016/j.socscimed.2020.113587.

Benson, T., Lavelle, F., McCloat, A., Mooney, E., Bucher, T., Egan, B., and Dean, M. (2018). The Impact of Nutrition and Health Claims on Consumer Perceptions and Portion Size Selection: Results from a Nationally Representative Survey. *Nutrients* 10 (5): 656. doi:10.3390/nu10050656.

Benson, T., Lavelle, F., McCloat, A., Mooney, E., Bucher, T., Egan, B., and Dean, M. (2019). Are the Claims to Blame? A Qualitative Study to Understand the Effects of Nutrition and Health Claims on Perceptions and Consumption of Food. *Nutrients* 11 (9): 2058. doi:10.3390/nu11092058.

Bentham, J. (1824/1987). *An introduction to the Principles of Morals and Legislation. In J. S. Mill and J. Bentham, Utilitarianism and Other Essays*. Harmondsworth: Penguin.

Berg, J., Dickhaut, J., and Mccabe, K. (1995). Trust, Reciprocity, and Social History. *Games and Economic Behavior* 10 (1): 122–42. doi:10.1006/game.1995.1027.

Bergeron, K. (2016). *Focus On: The Relevance of the Stage Heuristic Model for Developing Healthy Public Policies*. Toronto, ON: Queen's Printer for Ontario.

Bergeron, S., Doyon, M., Saulais, L., and Labrecque, J. A. (2019). Using Insights from Behavioral Economics to Nudge Individuals Towards Healthier Choices When Eating

Out: A Restaurant Experiment. *Food Quality and Preference* 73: 56-64. doi:10.1016/j.foodqual.2018.12.001.

Bevet, S., Niles M. T., and Pope, L. (2018). You Can't "Nudge" Nuggets: An Investigation of College Late-Night Dining with Behavioral Economics Interventions. *PLOS ONE* 13 (5): e0198162. doi:10.1371/journal.pone.0198162. eCollection 2018.

Biswas, D. (2009). The Effects of Option Framing on Consumer Choices: Making Decisions in Rational versus Experiential Processing Modes. *Journal of Consumer Behaviour* 8 (5): 284–99. doi:10doi:10.1002/cb.288.

Black, D. (1972). Reviewed Work: Law, Society, and Industrial Justice, by Philip Selznick, Philippe Nonet, Howard M. Vollmer. *American Journal of Sociology* 78 (3): 709–14. http://www.jstor.org/stable/2776321.

Blaga, O. (2017). Use And Effectiveness of Behavioural Economics in Interventions for Lifestyle Risk Factors of Non-Communicable Diseases: A Systematic Review with Policy Implications. *Perspect Public Health* 138 (2): 100–10. doi:10.1177/1757913917720233.

Bleasdale, J., Kruger, J., Gampp, A., Kurtz, K. and Anzman-Frasca, S. (2020). Examining Taste Testing and Point-Of-Purchase Prompting as Strategies to Promote Healthier Food Selection from Food Trucks. *Public Health Nutrition* 24 (4): 738-45. doi:10.1017/S1368980020002815.

Blom, S. S. A. H., Gillebaart, M., De Boer, F., van der Laan, N., De Ridder, Denise T. D. (2021). Under Pressure: Nudging Increases Healthy Food Choice in a Virtual Reality Supermarket, Irrespective of System 1 Reasoning. *Appetite* 160: 105116. doi:10.1016/j.appet.2021.105116.

Boehm, R., Read, M., Henderson, K., and Schwartz, M. (2020). Removing Competitive Foods v. Nudging and Marketing School Meals: A Pilot Study in High School Cafeterias. *Public Health Nutrition* 23 (2): 366-373. doi:10.1017/S136898001900329X.

Bohnet, I., Greig, F., Herrmann, B., and Zeckhauser, R. (2008). Betrayal Aversion: Evidence from Brazil, China, Oman, Switzerland, Turkey, and the United States. *American Economic Review* 98: 294–310. doi:10.1257/aer.98.1.294.

Britwum, K. and Yiannaka, A. (2019). Shaping Food Safety Perceptions: The Influence of Informational Nudges. *Journal of Behavioral and Experimental Economics* 81: 139–51. doi:10.1016/j.socec.2019.06.007.

Broers, V. J. V., Van den Broucke, S., Taverne, C., Luminet, O. (2019). Default-Name and Tasting Nudges Increase Salsify Soup Choice Without Increasing Overall Soup Choice. *Appetite* 138: 204-14. doi:10.1016/j.appet.2019.03.027.

Broers, V. J. V., De Breucker, C., Van den Broucke, S., and Luminet, O. (2017). A Systematic Review and Meta-Analysis of the Effectiveness of Nudging to Increase Fruit and Vegetable Choice. *European Journal of Public Health* 27: 912–20. doi:10.1093/eurpub/ckx085.

Brown, R. I. (1997). *Quality of Life of People with Disabilities*. Cheltenham: Nelson Thornes Ltd.

Bucher, T., Collins, C., Rollo, M. E., McCaffrey, T. A. et al. (2016). Nudging Consumers Towards Healthier Choices: A Systematic Review of Positional Influences on Food Choice. *British Journal of Nutrition* 115 (12): 2252–63. doi:10.1017/S0007114516001653.

Button, M. (2018). Bounded Rationality without Bounded Democracy: Nudges, Democratic Citizenship, and Pathways for Building Civic Capacity. *Perspectives on Politics* 16 (4): 1034–52. doi:10.1017/S1537592718002086.

Cadario, R. and Chandon, P. (2018) Which Healthy Eating Nudges Work Best? A Meta-Analysis of Field Experiments. *Marketing Science* 39 (3): 465–86. doi:10.1287/mksc.2018.1128.

Camerer, C. F. and Loewenstein, G. (2004). *Behavioral Economics: Past, Present, Future.* Princeton: Princeton University Press.

Cannan, E. (1901). Equity and Economy in Taxation. *The Economic Journal* 11 (44): 469–80. doi:10.2307/2957407.

Caraban, A., Karapanos, E., Goncalves, and D., Campos, P. (2019). 23 Ways to Nudge: A Review of Technology-Mediated Nudging in Human-Computer Interaction. *Chi 2019: Proceedings of the 2019 Chi Conference on Human Factors in Computing Systems*, Paper 503: 1–15. doi:10.1145/3290605.3300733.

Carroll, Kathryn A., Samek, A., and Zepeda, L. (2018). Food Bundling as a Health Nudge: Investigating Consumer Fruit and Vegetable Selection Using Behavioral Economics. *Appetite* 121: 237–48. doi:10.1016/j.appet.2017.11.082.

Carstensen, L. L. and Bailenson, J. N. (2011). Increasing Saving Behavior Through Age-Progressed Renderings of The Future Self. *Journal of Marketing Research* 48: 23–37. doi:10.1509/jmkr.48.SPL.S23.

Cartwright, E. (2011). *Behavioral Economics.* New York: Routledge.

Carver, C. S., Scheier, M. F., and Weintraub, J. K. (1989). Assessing Coping Strategies: A Theoretically Based Approach. *Journal Personality and Social Psychology* 56 (2) 267–83. doi:10.1037//0022-3514.56.2.267.

Castellari, E., Marette, S., Moro, D., and Sckokai, P. (2018). Can Menu Labeling Affect Away-From-Home Dietary Choices? *Bio-Based and Applied Economics* 7 (3): 249–63. doi:10.22004/ag.econ.301895.

Cerezo-Prieto M. and Frutos-Esteban, F. J. (2020). Impacto del Estilo de Vida de los Estudiantes Universitarios en la Promoción de Políticas Públicas en salud. El Caso de los Nudges [Impact of University Students Lifestyle in the Promotion of Public Health Policies. The Case of Nudges]. *Revista Española de Salud Pública* 94: e202007072.

Cerezo-Prieto, M. and Javier Frutos-Esteban, F. (2021). Hacia Rutas Saludables: Efecto de las Etiquetas Nutricionales en las Conductas Alimentarias en un Comedor Universitario [Towards Healthy Pathways: Effect of Nutrition Labels on Eating Behaviours in a University Canteen]. *Atención Primaria* 53 (5): 102022. doi:10.1016/j.aprim.2021.102022.

Chapman, L., Sadeghzadeh, C., Koutlas, M., Zimmer, C., and de Marco, M. (2019). Evaluation of Three Behavioural Economics 'Nudges' on Grocery and Convenience Store Sales of Promoted Nutritious Foods. *Public Health Nutrition* 22 (17): 3250–60. doi:10.1017/S1368980019001794.

Charry, K. and Tessitore, T. (2021). I Tweet, They Follow, You Eat: Number of Followers as Nudge on Social Media to Eat More Healthily. *Social Science & Medicine* 269: 113595. doi:10.1016/j.socscimed.2020.113595.

Chernev, A., Böckenholt, U., and Goodman, J. (2015). Choice Overload: A Conceptual Review and Meta-Analysis. *Journal of Consumer Psychology* 25 (2): 333–58. 10.1016/j.jcps.2014.08.002.

Chetty, R. (2015). Behavioral Economics and Public Policy: A Pragmatic Perspective. *American Economic Review* 105 (5): 1–33. doi:10.1257/aer.p20151108.

Cheung, T. T. L., Gillebaart, M., Kroese, F. M. et al. (2019). Cueing Healthier Alternatives for Take-Away: A Field Experiment on the Effects of (Disclosing) Three Nudges on Food Choices. *BMC Public Health* 19 (1): 974. doi:10.1186/s12889-019-7323-y.

Cialdini, R. B. (2008). *Influence: Science and Practice.* 5th ed. Boston: Pearson.

Cialdini, R. B. and Trost, M. R. (1998). Social Influence, Social Norms, Conformity and Compliance. In the *Handbook of Social Psychology*, edited by D. T. Gilbert, S. T. Fiske and G. Lindzey. 151–92. New York: McGraw-Hill.

Coffino, Jaime A., Udo, T., and Hormes, Julia M. (2020). Nudging while Online Grocery Shopping: A Randomized Feasibility Trial to Enhance Nutrition in Individuals with Food Insecurity. *Appetite* 152: 104714. doi:10.1016/j.appet.2020.104714.

Colby, H., Li, M., and Chapman, G. (2020). Dodging Dietary Defaults: Choosing Away from Healthy Nudges. *Organizational Behavior and Human Decision Processes* 61: 50–60. doi:10.1016/j.obhdp.2020.10.001.

Colson, G. and Grebitus, C. (2017). Relationship Between Children's BMI and Parents' Preferences for Kids' Yogurts with and without Front of Package Health Signals. *Agribusiness* 33 (2): 151–59. doi:10.1002/agr.21487.

Connelly, L. and Birch, S. (2020). Sustainability of Publicly Funded Health Care Systems: What Does Behavioural Economics Offer? *Pharmacoeconomics* 38 (12): 1289–95. doi:10.1007/s40273-020-00955-x.

Coucke, N., Vermeir, I., Slabbinck, H., and Van Kerckhove, A. (2019). Show Me More! The Influence of Visibility on Sustainable Food Choices. *Foods* 8 (6): 186. doi:10.3390/foods8060186.

Coulter, K. S. and Coulter, R. A. (2005). Size Does Matter: The Effects of Magnitude Representation Congruency on Price Perceptions and Purchase Likelihood. *Journal of Consumer Psychology* 15 (1): 64–76. doi:10.1207/s15327663jcp1501_9.

Crossman, A. (2021). Folkways, Mores, Taboos, and Laws. *Thoughtco*. https://www.thoughtco.com/folkways-mores-taboos-and-laws-3026267 (accessed August 27, 2023).

Dalrymple, J. C., Radnitz, C., Loeb, and Keller, K. L. (2020). Optimal Defaults as a Strategy to Improve Selections from Children's Menus in Full-Service Theme Park Dining. *Appetite* 152:104697. doi:10.1016/j.appet.2020.104697.

De Marchi, E., Cavaliere, A., Nayga, R. M., and Banterle, A. (2020). Incentivizing Vegetable Consumption in School-Aged Children: Evidence from A Field Experiment. *J Consum Aff* 54 (1): 261–85. doi:10.1111/joca.12268.

Detweiler, J. B., Bedell, B. T., Salovey, P., Pronin, E., and Rothman, A. J. (1999). Message Framing and Sunscreen Use: Gain-Framed Messages Motivate Beach-Goers. *Health Psychology* 18 (2): 189–96. doi:10.1037//0278-6133.18.2.189.

Diclemente, C. C., Prochaska, J. O., and Gibertini, M. (1985). Self-Efficacy and the Stages of Self-Change of Smoking. *Cognitive Therapy and Research* 9 (2): 181–200. doi:10.1007/BF01204849.

Ding, D., Cruz, B. D., Green, M. A., and Bauman, A. E. (2020). Is the Covid-19 Lockdown Nudging People to Be More Active: A Big Data Analysis. *British Journal of Sports Medicine* 54 (20): 1183–4. doi:10.1136/bjsports-2020-102575.

Djupegot, I. L. (2019). Investigating Young Adults' Perceived Effectiveness of Textual Information About Food-Related Nudging. *British Food Journal* 122 (2): 489–502. doi:10.1108/BFJ-08-2019-0649.

Dolan, P., Hallsworth, M., Halpern, D., King, D., and Vlaev, I. (2010). *Mindspace: Influencing Behaviour Through Public Policy*. Institute for Government. https://www.instituteforgovernment.org.uk/sites/default/files/publications/MINDSPACE.pdf.

Dolgopolova, I., Toscano, A., Roosen, J. (2021). Different Shades of Nudges: Moderating Effects of Individual Characteristics and States on the Effectiveness of Nudges During a Fast-Food Order. *Sustainability* 13 (23): 13347. doi:10.3390/su132313347.

Dos Santos, Q., Nogueira, B. M., Rodrigues, V. M., et al. (2018). Nudging Using the 'Dish of The Day' Strategy Does Not Work for Plant-Based Meals in a Danish Sample of Adolescent and Older People. *Int J Consum Stud*. 42: 327–34. doi:10.1111/ijcs.12421.

Dos Santos, Q., Perez-Cueto, F. J. A., Rodrigues, V. M. et al. (2020). Impact of a Nudging Intervention and Factors Associated with Vegetable Dish Choice Among European Adolescents. *Eur J Nutr* 59 (1): 231–47. doi:10.1007/s00394-019-01903-y.

Elmore, R. F. (1987). Instruments and Strategy in Public Policy. *Review of Policy Research* 7 (1): 174-86. doi:10.1111/j.1541-1338.1987.tb00036.x.

Emoto N., Soga A., Fukuda I., Tanimura-Inagaki K. et al. (2020). Irrational Responses to Risk Preference Questionnaires by Patients with Diabetes with or without Retinopathy and Comparison with Those without Diabetes. *Diabetes Metab Syndr Obes* 13: 4961-71. doi:10.2147/DMSO.S283591.

Enden G. Van Den and Geyskens K. (2021). Attract The Best: The Attraction Effect as an Effective Strategy to Enhance Healthy Choices. *PLOS ONE* 16 (11): e0259521. doi:10.1371/journal.pone.0259521.

Erjavec, M., Williams, S., Viktor, S. et al. (2020) Nudge with Caution: Targeting Fruit and Vegetable Consumption in Primary Schools. *Eur J Clin Nutr* 75 (4): 724-7. doi:10.1038 /s41430-020-00772-7.

Ewert, B. (2017). Promoting Health in Schools: Theoretical Reflections on the Settings Approach Versus Nudge Tactics. *Soc Theory Health* 15: 430-447. doi:10.1057 /s41285-017-0036-3.

Falk, A. (2007). Gift Exchange in The Field. *The Econometric Society* 75 (5): 1501 -11. http://www.jstor.org/stable/4502037.

Feldstein, Paul J. (1999). *Health Care Economics*. 5th ed. Albany, NY: Delmar Publishers.

Fennis, B. M., Gineikiene, J., Barauskaite, D., and van Koningsbruggen, G M. (2020). Nudging Health: Scarcity Cues Boost Healthy Consumption Among Fast Rather Than Slow Strategists (and Abundance Cues Do the Opposite). *Food Quality and Preference* 85: 103967. doi:10.1016/j.foodqual.2020.103967.

Ferrer R., Orehek E., Scheier, M. F., and O'Connell M. E. (2018). Cigarette Tax Rates, Behavioral Disengagement, and Quit Ratios Among Daily Smokers. *Journal of Economic Psychology* 66: 13–21. doi:10.1016/j.joep.2018.03.005.

Filimonau, V., Lemmer, Ch., Marshall, D., and Bejjani, G. (2017). Nudging' As an Architect of More Responsible Consumer Choice in Food Service Provision: The Role of Restaurant Menu Design. *Journal of Cleaner Production* 144: 161–170. doi:10.1016 /j.jclepro.2017.01.010.

Filimonau, V. and Krivcova, M. (2017). Restaurant Menu Design and More Responsible Consumer Food Choice: An Exploratory Study of Managerial Perceptions. *Journal of Cleaner Production* 143:516–27. doi:10.1016/j.jclepro.2016.12.080.

Fisher, F. (2018). Nutrition Labeling Reduces Valuations of Food Through Multiple Health and Taste Channels. *Appetite* 120: 500–04. doi:10.1016/j.appet.2017.09.013.

Fitzgerald S., Geaney F., Perry I. (2019). P66 Taking Nudge Digital with Food Choice at Work: from Evaluation to Practical Application in Everyday Workplace Settings. *Epidemiol Community Health* 73 (1): 101–2. doi:10.1136/jech-2019-SSMabstracts.217.

Flores, D., Reimann, M., Castaño, R., and Lopez, A. (2019). If I Indulge First, I Will Eat Less Overall: The Unexpected Interaction Effect of Indulgence and Presentation Order on Consumption. *Journal of Experimental Psychology: Applied* 25 (2): 162–76. doi:10.1037/xap0000210.

Fogg, B. J. (2009). The Behavior Grid: 35 Ways Behavior Can Change. *Persuasive* 42: 1–5. doi:10.1145/1541948.1542001.

Frederick, S. and Loewenstein, G. (1999). Hedonic Adaptation. In *Well-Being: The Foundations of Hedonic Psychology*, edited by D. Kahneman, E. Diener, and N. Schwarz, 302–29. New York: Russell Sage Foundation.

Frederick, S., Loewenstein, G., and O'Donoghue, T. (2002). Time Discounting and Time Preference: A Critical Review. *Journal Of Economic Literature* 40 (2): 351–401. doi:10.1257/002205102320161311.

Friis R., Skov, L. R., Olsen, A., Appleton, K. M., Saulais L., Dinnella C., et al. (2017). Comparison of Three Nudge Interventions (Priming, Default Option, and Perceived Variety) to Promote Vegetable Consumption in a Self-Service Buffet Setting. *PLOS ONE* 12 (5): e0176028. doi:10.1371/journal.pone.0176028.

Fudenberg, D. (2006). Advancing Beyond Advances in Behavioral Economics. *Journal of Economic Literature* 44 (3): 694–711. doi:10.1257/jel.44.3.694.

Furth-Matzkin, M. and Sunstein, C. R. (2018). Social Influences on Policy Preferences: Conformity and Reactance. *Minnesota Law Review*, 1339–79. doi:10.2139/ssrn.2816595.

Garnett, E. E., Balmford, A., Sandbrook, Ch., Pilling, M. A., and Marteau, T. M. (2019). Impact of Increasing Vegetarian Availability on Meal Selection and Sales in Cafeterias. *Proceedings of the National Academy of Sciences of the United States of America* 116 (42): 20923–9. doi:10.1073/pnas.1907207116.

Gestel van, L. C., Kroese, F. M. and De Ridder, D. T. D. (2017). Nudging at the Checkout Counter – A Longitudinal Study of The Effect of a Food Repositioning Nudge on Healthy Food Choice. *Psychology and Health* 33 (6): 800-9. doi:10.1080/08870446.2017 .1416116.

Gestel van, L. C., Adriaanse, M. A. and De Ridder, D. T. D. (2020). Beyond Discrete Choices – Investigating the Effectiveness of a Proximity Nudge with Multiple Alternative Options. *Frontiers in Psychology* 11: 1211. doi:10.3389/fpsyg.2020.01211.

Ghoniem, A., Van Dillen, L. F., and Hofmann, W. (2020). Choice Architecture Meets Motivation Science: How Stimulus Availability Interacts with Internal Factors in Shaping the Desire for Food. *Appetite* 155:104815. doi:10.1016/j.appet.2020.104815.

Glaeser, E., Laibson, D., Scheinkman, J., and Soutter, C. (2000). Measuring Trust. *The Quarterly Journal of Economics* 115 (3): 811–46. doi.org/10.1162/003355300554926.

Golapan, M. and Pirog, M. A. (2017). Applying Behavioral Insights in Policy Analysis: Recent Trends in the United States. *Policy Studies Journal* 45 (1): 82–114. doi:10.1111 /psj.12202.

Golman, R., Hagmann, D., and Loewenstein, G. (2017). Information Avoidance. *Journal Of Economic Literature* 55 (1): 96–135. doi:10.1257/jel.20151245.

Gong, C. L., Zangwill, K. M., Hay, J. W. et al. (2019). Behavioral Economics Interventions to Improve Outpatient Antibiotic Prescribing for Acute Respiratory Infections: A Cost-Effectiveness Analysis. *Journal of General Internal Medicine* 34 (6): 846–54. doi:10.1007/s11606-018-4467-x.

Gonçalves, D., Coelho, P., Martinez, L. F., Monteiro, P. (2021). Nudging Consumers Toward Healthier Food Choices: A Field Study on the Effect of Social Norms. *Sustainability* 13:1660. doi:10.3390/su13041660.

Goodwin, T. (2012). Why We Should Reject 'Nudge'. *Politics* 32 (2): 85–92. doi:10.1111 /j.1467-9256.2012.01430.x.

Gouldner, A. W. (1960). The Norm of Reciprocity: A Preliminary Statement. *American Sociological Review* 25 (2): 161–178. doi:10.2307/2092623.

Grebitus, C., Roscoe, R. D., Van Loo, E. J., and Kula, I. (2020). Sustainable Bottled Water: How Nudging and Internet Search Affect Consumers' Choices. *Journal of Cleaner Production* 267:121930. doi:10.1016/j.jclepro.2020.121930.

Griesoph, A., Hoffmann, S., Merk, C., Rehdanz, K., and Schmidt, U. (2021). Guess What ...? – How Guessed Norms Nudge Climate-Friendly Food Choices in Real-Life Settings. *Sustainability* 13 (15): 8669. doi:10.3390/su13158669.

Grinblatt, M. and Keloharju, M. (2009). Sensation Seeking, Overconfidence, and Trading Activity. *The Journal of Finance* 64 (2): 549–78. doi:10.1111/j.1540-6261.2009.01443.x.

Grutzmacher, S. K., Duru, E. Braunscheidel, Speirs, K. E., and Worthington, L. (2018). Using Text Messages to Engage Low-Income Parents in School-Based Nutrition

Education. *Journal of Hunger and Environmental Nutrition* 13 (3): 335–39. doi:10.1080 /19320248.2017.1364196.

Guo, N., Wang, J., Nicholas, S., Maitland, E. and Zhu, D. W. (2020). Behavioral Differences in the Preference for Hepatitis B Virus. Vaccination: A Discrete Choice Experiment. *Vaccines* 8 (3): 527. doi:10.3390/vaccines8030527.

Gurková, E. (2011). Hodnocení kvality života [Assessment of quality of life]. Prague: Grada.

Gustafson, Ch. R. and Zeballos, E. (2020). The Effect of Presenting Relative Calorie Information on Calories Ordered. *Appetite* 153:104727. doi:10.1016/j.appet.2020.104727.

Hagmann, D., Siegrist, M. and Hartmann, C. (2018). Taxes, Labels, or Nudges? Public Acceptance of Various Interventions Designed to Reduce Sugar Intake. *Food Policy* 79:156–165. doi:10.1016/j.foodpol.2018.06.008.

Hall, E. E., Ekkekakis, P. and Petruzzello, S. J. (2002). The Affective Beneficence of Vigorous Exercise Revisited. *British Journal of Health Psychology* 7: 47–66. doi:10.1348/13591070216935.

Halpern, D. and Sanders, M. (2016). Nudging By Government: Progress, Impact and Lessons Learnt. *Behavioral Science & Policy* 2 (2): 52–65. doi:10.1353/bsp.2016.0015.

Halpern, D. (2016). *Inside The Nudge Unit: How Small Changes Can Make a Big Difference.* London: WH Allen.

Haluzík, M. (2013). *Praktická léčba diabetu* [Practical treatment of diabetes]. 2nd ed. Prague: Mladá Fronta.

Hamdi, N., Ellison, B., Mccaffrey, J., Metcalfe, J. J., Hoffman, A. et al. (2020). Implementation of a Multi-Component School Lunch Environmental Change Intervention to Improve Child Fruit and Vegetable Intake: A Mixed-Methods Study. *Int. J. Environ. Res. Public Health* 17 (11): 3971. 10.3390/ijerph17113971.

Hansen, P. G., Schilling, M. and Malthesen, M. S. (2021) Nudging Healthy and Sustainable Food Choices: Three Randomized Controlled Field Experiments Using a Vegetarian Lunch-Default as a Normative Signal. *J Public Health (Oxf)* 43 (2): 392–7. doi:10.1093/pubmed/fdz154.

Harbers, M. C., Middel, C. N. H., Stuber, J. M., Beulens, J. W. J., Rutters, F., and Van Der Schouw, Y. T. (2021). Determinants of Food Choice and Perceptions of Supermarket-Based Nudging Interventions Among Adults with Low Socioeconomic Position: The Supreme Nudge Project. *Int. J. Environ. Res. Public Health* 18 (11): 6175. doi:10.3390 /ijerph18116175.

Harris, D. (2013). *The Rational Consumer on the Checkout.* Tribal Insight (blog). Wordpress. March 29, 2013. https://tribalinsight.wordpress.com/2013/03/29/the-rational-consumer-on-the-checkout/.

Hartford, T. (2009). To Nudge Is One Thing, to Nanny Quite Another. *Financial Times.* September 19, 2009, https://www.ft.com/content/ac77105a-a0f5-11de-a88d -00144feabdc0.

Häubl, G., Larrick, R. P., Payne, J. W., Peters, E., Schkade, D., Wansink, B., and Weber, E. U. (2012), Beyond Nudges: Tools of a Choice Architecture. *Marketing Letters* 23: 487–504. doi: org/10.1007/s11002-012-9186-1.

Hausman, D. M. and Welch, B. (2010). Debate: to Nudge or Not to Nudge. *The Journal of Political Philosophy* 18 (1): 123–136. doi:10.1111/j.1467-9760.2009.00351.x.

Haynos, A. and Roberto, C. (2017). The Effects of Restaurant Menu Calorie Labeling on Hypothetical Meal Choices of Females with Disordered Eating. *Int J Eat Disord* 50 (3): 275–83. doi:10.1002/eat.22675.

Hawkins, L., Farrow, C., and Thomas, J. M. (2021). Does Exposure to Socially Endorsed Food Images on Social Media Influence Food Intake? *Appetite* 165: 105424. doi:10.1016/j.appet.2021.105424.

Hendl, J. (2005). *Kvalitativní výzkum: Základní metody a aplikace* [Qualitative research: Basic Methods and Applications]. Prague: Portál.

Hershfield, H. E., Goldstein D. G., Sharpe, W. F., Fox, J. et al. (2011). Increasing Saving Behavior Through Age-Progressed Renderings of The Future Self. *Journal of Marketing Research* 48: 23–37. doi:10.1509/jmkr.48.SPL.S23.

Hilbert, M. (2012). Toward a Synthesis of Cognitive Biases: How Noisy Information Processing Can Bias Human Decision Making. *Psychological Bulletin* 138 (2): 211–37. doi:10.1037/a0025940.

Hirshleifer, D., and G. Y. Luo (2001). On the Survival of Overconfident Traders in a Competitive Securities Market. *Journal of Financial Markets* 4 (1): 73–84. doi:10.1016/S1386-4181(00)00014-8.

Hoenink, Jc., Mackenbach, Jd., Waterlander, W., Lakerveld, J., Van Der Laan, N., Beulens, Jwj. (2020). The Effects of Nudging and Pricing on Healthy Food Purchasing Behavior in a Virtual Supermarket Setting: A Randomized Experiment. *International Journal of Behavioral Nutrition and Physical Activity* 17: 98. doi:10.1186/s12966-020-01005-7.

Hoenink, J. C., Stuber, J. M., Lakerveld, J. et al. (2021). The Effect of On-Shelf Sugar Labeling on Beverage Sales in The Supermarket: A Comparative Interrupted Time Series Analysis of a Natural Experiment. *International Journal of Behavioral Nutrition and Physical Activity* 18 (1): 49. doi:10.1186/s12966-021-01114-x.

Hogreve, J., Matta, S., Hettich, A. S., and Reczek, R. W. (2020). How Do Social Norms Influence Parents' Food Choices for Their Children? The Role of Social Comparison and Implicit Self-Theories. *Journal of Retailing.* doi:10.1016/J.Jretai.2020.05.002.

Hohenstein, N. O., Feisel, E. and Hartmann, E. (2014). Human Resource Management Issues in Supply Chain Management Research: A Systematic Literature Review from 1998 to 2014. *International Journal of Physical Distribution and Logistics Management* 44 (6): 434–463. doi:10.1108/IJPDLM-06-2013-0175.

Holligan, S., Yi, S., Kanetkar, V., Haines, J., Dergham, J., Royall, D., and Brauer, P. (2019). Preferences for Vegetables Among University Foodservice Users: A Survey to Inform Nudge-Based Interventions. *British Food Journal* 121 (12): 3338–49. doi:10.1108/BFJ-09-2018-0597.

Howlett M. and Ramesh, M. (1993). Patterns of Policy Instrument Choice: Policy Styles, Policy Learning and the Privatization Experience. *Review of Policy Research* 12 (1–2): 3–24. doi:10.1111/j.1541-1338.1993.tb00505.x.

Howlett, M. and Ramesh, M. (1995). *Studying Public Policy: Policy Cycles and Policy Subsystems.* Oxford: Oxford University Press.

Huf, S., Kerrison R. S., King, D., Chadborn, T. et al. (2020). Behavioral Economics Informed Message Content in Text Message Reminders to Improve Cervical Screening Participation: Two Pragmatic Randomized Controlled Trials. *Preventive Medicine* 139:106170. doi:10.1016/j.ypmed.2020.106170.

Huitink, M., Poelman, M. P., Van Den Eynde, E., Seidell, J. C., and Dijkstra, S. C. (2020). Social Norm Nudges in Shopping Trolleys to Promote Vegetable Purchases: A Quasi-Experimental Study in a Supermarket in a Deprived Urban Area in The Netherlands. *Appetite* 151: 104655. doi:10.1016/j.appet.2020.104655.

Hunt, M. M. (2007). *The Story of Psychology.* New York: Anchor Books.

Immink, V., Kornelis, M., and Van Kleef, E. (2021). Vegetable Interventions at Unconventional Occasions: The Effect of Freely Available Snack Vegetables at

Workplace Meetings on Consumption. *International Journal of Workplace Health Management* 14 (4): 426–39. doi:10.1108/IJWHM-06-2020-0108.

Iyengar, S. S. and Lepper, M. (2000). When Choice Is Demotivating: Can One Desire Too Much of a Good Thing? *Journal of Personality and Social Psychology* 79 (6): 995–1006. doi:10.1037/0022-3514.79.6.995.

Jinghui Hou (2017). Can Interface Cues Nudge Modeling of Food Consumption? Experiments on a Food-Ordering Website. *Journal of Computer-Mediated Communication* 22 (4): 196–214. doi:10.1111/jcc4.12190.

Joffe, M. (2017). Mechanism in Behavioural Economics. *Journal of Economic Methodology* 26 (3): 228–42. doi:10.1080/1350178X.2019.1625214.

Johnson, E. J. and Goldstein, D. G. (2004). Defaults and Donation Decisions. *Transplantation* 78 (12): 1713–6. doi:10.1097/01.tp.0000149788.10382.b2.

Just, D. R., Okello, J. J., Gabrielyan, G. et al. (2021). A Behavioral Intervention Increases Consumption of a New Biofortified Food by School Children: Evidence from a Field Experiment in Nigeria. *Eur J Dev Res* 34:124–146. doi:10.1057/s41287-021-00363-7.

Kahneman, D., Knetsch, J. L., and Thaler, R. H. (1991). Anomalies: The Endowment Effect, Loss Aversion, and Status Quo Bias. *Journal of Economic Perspectives* 5 (1): 193–206. doi:10.1257/jep.5.1.193.

Kahneman, D. (2003). Maps of Bounded Rationality: Psychology for Behavioral Economics. *The American Economic Review* 93 (5): 1449–75.

Kahneman, D. (2011). *Thinking, Fast and Slow.* London: Allen Lane.

Kahneman, D. and Frederick, S. (2002). Representativeness Revisited: Attribute Substitution in Intuitive Judgment. In *Heuristics of Intuitive Judgement: Extensions and Applications*, edited by T. Gilovich, D. Griffin, and D. Kahneman, 49–81. New York: Cambridge University Press.

Kahneman, D., and Tversky, A. (1999). Evaluation by Moments: Past and Future. In *Choices, Values and Frames*, edited by D. Kahneman and A. Tversky, 2–23. New York: Cambridge University Press.

Kahneman, D. and Frederick, S. (2002). Representativeness Revisited: Attribute Substitution in Intuitive Judgment. Heuristics and Biases. In *The Psychology of Intuitive Judgment*, edited by Thomas Gilovich, Dale Griffin, and Daniel Kahneman, 49–81. Cambridge: Cambridge University Press. doi:10.1017/CBO9780511808098.004.

Kahneman, D., Knetsch, J. L., and Thaler, R. H. (1990). Experimental Tests of the Endowment Effect and the Coase Theorem. *Journal of Political Economy* 98 (6): 1325–48. doi:10.1086/261737.

Kahneman, D., Knetsch, J. L., and Thaler, R. H. (1991). Anomalies: The Endowment Effect, Loss Aversion, and Status Quo Bias. *Journal of Economic Perspectives* 5 (1): 193–206.

Kalnická, V. (2019). *Výdaje na zdravotní péči jsou v porovnání s EU nízké* [Healthcare spending is low compared to the EU], Statistika&My, published June 20, 2019, https://www.statistikaamy.cz/2019/06/20/vydaje-na-zdravotni-peci-jsou-v-porovnani-s-eu-nizke.

Karlsson, N., Loewenstein, G., and D. Seppi (2009). The Ostrich Effect: Selective Attention to Information. *Journal of Risk and Uncertainty* 38:95–115. doi:10.1007/s11166-009-9060-6.

Kawa, C., Ianiro-Dahm, P. M., Nijhuis, J. F. H., and Gijselaers, W. H. (2021). Cafeteria Online: Nudges for Healthier Food Choices in a University Cafeteria – A Randomized Online Experiment. *Int. J. Environ. Res. Public Health* 18 (24): 12924. doi:10.3390/ijerph182412924.

Keane, Michael P., Ketcham, Jonathan D., Kuminoff, Nicolai V., and Neal, T. (2020). Evaluating Consumers' Choices of Medicare Part D Plans. *Behavioral Welfare Economics* 222 (1): 107–40. doi:10.3386/W25652.

Keegan, E., Kemps, E., Prichard I., Polivy, J., Herman, Peter C., and Tiggemann, M. (2019). The Effect of The Spatial Positioning of a Healthy Food Cue on Food Choice from a Pictorial-Style Menu. *Eating Behaviors* 34:101313. doi:10.1016/j.eatbeh.2019 .101313.

Kim, J., Hwang, E., Park, J., Lee, J. C., and Park, J. (2019). Position Effects of Menu Item Displays in Consumer Choices: Comparisons of Horizontal Versus Vertical Displays. *Cornell Hospitality Quarterly* 60 (2): 116–24. doi:10.1177/1938965518778234.

Klazar, S. (2010). Behavioral Consequences of Optimal Tax Structure – Empirical Analysis. *European Financial and Accounting Journal* 5 (1): 51–63. doi:10.18267/j.efaj.44.

Klazar, S. and Maaytová, A. (2013). An Evaluation of Public Contracts in Teaching Hospitals in the Czech Republic in the Years from 2006 to 2011. In *Finance and The Performance of Firms in Science, Education, and Practice – Proceedings of the 6th International Scientific Conference Univerzita Tomáše Bati in Zlín, 25.04.2013–26.04.2013*, edited by E. Jirčíková, A. Knápková, E. Pastuszková, 348–357. Zlín: Univerzita Tomáše Bati ve Zlíně.

Klazar, S. and Maaytová, A. (2013). Public Contracts in Hospitals in Czech Republic Revised. In *Creating Global Competitive Economies. 2020 Vision Planning & Implementation* [CD ROM], edited by Khalid S. Soliman. Rome: International Business Information Management Association (Ibima): 602–609.

Kleef, E. Van, Kremer, F., and Van Trijp, H. C. M. (2020). The Impact of a Gradual Healthier Assortment Among Vocational Schools Participating in a School Canteen Programme: Evidence from Sales and Student Survey Data. *International Journal of Environmental Research and Public Health* 17 (12): 1–16. doi:10.3390/Ijerph17124352

Kleef, E. Van, Seijdell, K., Vingerhoeds, Monique H., De Wijk, R. A., and Van Trijp H. C. M. (2018). The Effect of a Default-Based Nudge on The Choice of Whole Wheat Bread. *Appetite* 21: 179-85. doi:10.1016/j.appet.2017.11.091.

Knowles, D., Brown, K., and Aldrovandi, S. (2019). Exploring the Underpinning Mechanisms of the Proximity Effect within a Competitive Food Environment. *Appetite* 134: 94–102. doi:10.1016/j.appet.2018.12.005.

Kosīte, D., König, L. M., De-Loyde, K. et al. (2019). Plate Size and Food Consumption: A Pre-Registered Experimental Study in a General Population Sample. *Int J Behav Nutr Phys Act* 16 (1): 75. doi:10.1186/s12966-019-0826-1.

Kotarbiński, T. (1972). *Praxeologie*. Prague: Academia.

Kraak, V. I., Englund, T., Misyak, S., and Serrano, E. L. (2017). A Novel Marketing Mix and Choice Architecture Framework to Nudge Restaurant Customers Toward Healthy Food Environments to Reduce Obesity in the United States. *Obesity Reviews* 18 (8): 852–68. doi:10doi:10.1111/obr.12553.

Krämer, W. (2014). Book review on D. Kahneman (2011): Thinking, Fast and Slow. *Stat Papers* 55 (3): 915. doi:10.1007/s00362-013-0533-y.

Krebs, V. et al. (2015). *Sociální politika* [Social policy]. 6th ed., Prague: Wolters Kluwer.

Krpan, D., Galizzi, Matteo M., and Dolan, P. (2019). Looking at Spillovers in the Mirror: Making a Case for Behavioral Spillunders. *Frontiers in Psychology* 10: 1142. doi:10.3389 /fpsyg.2019.01142.

Krpan, D. and Houtsma, N. (2020). To Veg or Not to Veg? The Impact of Framing on Vegetarian Food Choice. *Journal of Environmental Psychology* 67: 101391. doi:10.1016 /j.jenvp.2020.101391.

Kuehnhanss, C. (2018) The Challenges of Behavioural Insights for Effective Policy Design. *Policy and Society* 38 (1): 14–40. doi:10.1080/14494035.2018.1511188

Kuhn, S. T. (1970). *The Structure of Scientific Revolutions*. Chicago: The University of Chicago.

Kurz, V. (2018). Nudging to Reduce Meat Consumption: Immediate and Persistent Effects of An Intervention at a University Restaurant. *Journal of Environmental Economics and Management* 90: 317–341. doi:10.1016/J.Jeem.2018.06.005.

Labbe, D., Fries, R. L., Ferrage, A., Lenfant, F., Godinot, N., and Martin, N. (2018). Right Sizing: Sensory-Based Product Design Is a Promising Strategy to Nudge Consumers Toward Healthier Portions. *Nutrients* 10 (10): 1544. doi:10.3390/nu10101544.

Lai, C.-Y., List, J. A., and A. Samek (2020). Got Milk? Using Nudges to Reduce Consumption of Added Sugar. *American Journal of Agricultural Economics, John Wiley and Sons* 102 (1): 154–68. doi:10.1093/ajae/aaz022.

Laibson, D. (1997). Golden Eggs and Hyperbolic Discounting. *Quarterly Journal of Economics* 112: 443–477. doi:10.1162/003355397555253.

Lange, Ch., Schwartz, C., Hachefa, C., Cornil, Y., Nicklaus, S., and Chandon, P. (2020). Portion Size Selection in Children: Effect of Sensory Imagery for Snacks Varying in Energy Density. *Appetite* 150: 104656. doi:10.1016/j.appet.2020.104656.

Lean, M. E. J., Leslie, W., Barnes, A. C. et al. (2018). Primary Care-Led Weight Management for Remission of Type Diabetes. (Direct): An Open-Label, Cluster-Randomised Trial. *The Lancet* 391 (10120): 541–51. doi:10.1016/S0140-6736(17)33102-1.

Lepenies, R., Mackay, K., and Quigley, M. (2018). Three Challenges for Behavioural Science and Policy: The Empirical, the Normative and the Political. *Behavioural Public Policy* 2(2): 174–82. doi:10.1017/bpp.2018.18.

Levine, David K. (2012). *Is Behavioral Economics Doomed? The Ordinary Versus the Extraordinary*. Cambridge: Open Book Publishers.

Linhart, J., Petrusek, M. et al. (1996). *Velký sociologický slovník* [The Great Sociological Dictionary]. Prague: Karolinum.

Loeb, K. L., Radnitz, C., Keller, K. L., Schwartz, M. B., et al. (2018). The Application of Optimal Defaults to Improve Elementary School Lunch Selections: Proof of Concept. *J School Health* 88: 265–71. doi:10.1111/josh.12611.

Loeb, K. L., Radnitz, C., Keller, K., Schwartz, B. Marlene, Marcus, S., Pierson, N. R., Shannon, M., and Delaurentis, D. (2017). The Application of Defaults to Optimize Parents' Health-Based Choices for Children. *Appetite* 113: 368–75. doi:10.1016/j.appet.2017.02.039.

Loewenstein, G. (1999). A Visceral Account of Addiction. In *Editors Getting Hooked: Rationality and Addiction*, edited by J. Elster, O. J. Skog, 235–64. New York: Cambridge University Press.

Loewenstein G., Asch, D. Friedman J. et al. (2012) Can Behavioural Economics Make Us Healthier? *BMJ* (May 23): 344. doi:10.1136/bmj.e3482.

Loewenstein, G. (2000). Emotions in Economic Theory and Economic Behavior. *American Economic Review* 90 (2): 426–32. doi:10.1257/Aer.90.2.426.

Loewenstein, G., Weber, E. U., Hsee, C. K., and Welch, N. (2001). Risk as Feelings. *Psychological Bulletin* 127 (2): 267–86. doi:10.1037/0033-2909.127.2.267.

Lourenco, J. S., Ciriolo, E., Almeida, S. R., and Troussard, X. (2016). Behavioural Insights Applied to Policy: European Report. *Jrc Science Hub*. doi:10.2760/903938.

Maaytová, A., Gajdošová E., and Láchová, L. (2018). Změny v demografické struktuře a výdaje na zdravotnictví České Republiky [Changes in the demografic structure in the Czech republic]. *Český finanční a účetní časopis* 4: 19–31. doi:10.18267/j.cfuc.521.

Maaytová, A. and Klazar, S. (2014). Competitive Effect in Czech Hospitals. In *Proceeding of the 19th International Conference Theoretical and Practical Aspests of Public Finance 2014. Prague, 11.04.2014–12.04.2014*, edited by L. Sedmihradská, 165–71. Prague: Wolters Kluwer.

Madrian, B. C. (2014). Applying Insights from Behavioral Economics to Policy Design. *Annual Review of Economics* 6 (1): 663–88. doi:10.1146/annurev-economics-080213 -041033.

Madrian, B. and D. Shea (2001). The Power of Suggestion: Inertia in 401(K) Participation and Savings Behavior. *Quarterly Journal of Economics* 116: 1149–87. http://www.jstor.org /stable/2696456.

Magdaleno, L., Rolling, T., Galia S. W., and Ayala Guadalupe X. (2021) Evaluation of a Front-of-Pack Food Labeling Intervention on a College Campus. *Journal of American College Health* (Sept 14): 1–9. doi:10.1080/07448481.2021.1970563.

Maheswaran, D., Mackie, D. M., and Chaiken, S. (1992). Brand Name as a Heuristic Cue: The Effects of Task Importance and Expectancy Confirmation on Consumer Judgments. *Journal of Consumer Psychology* 1 (4): 317–36. doi:10.1016/S1057-7408(08) 80058-7.

Mai, R. and Hoffmann, S. (2017). Indirect Ways to Foster Healthier Food Consumption Patterns: Health-Supportive Side Effects of Health-Unrelated Motives. *Food Quality and Preference* 57: 54–68. doi:10.1016/j.foodqual.2016.11.009.

Maltz, A. and Sarid, A. (2020). Attractive Flu Shot: A Behavioral Approach to Increasing Influenza Vaccination Uptake Rates. *Med Decis Making* 40 (6): 774–84. doi:10.1177/0272989X20944190.

Malý, I. (1998) *Problém optimální alokace zdrojů ve zdravotnictví* [The Problem of Optimal Allocation of Resources in Healthcare]. Brno: Masarykova Univerzita.

Manippa, V., Giuliani, F., and Brancucci, A. (2020). Healthiness or Calories? Side Biases in Food Perception and Preference. *Appetite* 147: 104552. doi:10.1016/j.appet.2019 .104552.

Marcano-Olivier, M., Pearson, R., Ruparell, A. et al. (2019). A Low-Cost Behavioural Nudge and Choice Architecture Intervention Targeting School Lunches Increases Children's Consumption of Fruit: A Cluster Randomised Trial. *Int J Behav Nutr Phys Act* 16:20. doi:10.1186/s12966-019-0773-x.

March, J. G. (1978). Bounded Rationality, Ambiguity, and the Engineering of Choice. *The Bell Journal of Economics* 9 (2): 587–608. doi:10.2307/3003600.

Marques, I. C. F., Ting, M., Cedillo-Martínez, D., and Pérez-Cueto, F. J. (2020). Effect of Impulsivity Traits on Food Choice Within a Nudging Intervention. *Nutrients* 12 (5): 1402. doi:10.3390/nu12051402.

Martin, S. J., Bassi, S. and Dunbar-Rees, R. (2012). Commitments, Norms and Custard Creams – A Social Influence Approach to Reducing Did Not Attends (DNAS). *Journal of The Royal Society of Medicine* 105 (3): 101–4. doi:10.1258/jrsm.2011.110250.

Martin-Moreno, J. M., Ruiz-Segovia, N. and Diaz-Rubio, E. (2020). Behavioural and Structural Interventions in Cancer Prevention: Towards the 2030 SDG Horizon. *Molecular Oncology* 15 (3): 801–8. doi: 10.1002/1878-0261.12805.

Mathis, K. (2016). *Nudging – Possibilities, Limitations and Applications in European Law and Economics*. New York: Springer.

Mazar, N. and Ariely, D. (2006). Dishonesty in Everyday Life and Its Policy Implications. *Journal of Public Policy & Marketing* 25 (1): 117–26. doi:10.1509/jppm.25.1.117.

Mazar, N., Amir, O., and Ariely, D. (2008). The Dishonesty of Honest People: A Theory of Self-Concept Maintenance. *Journal of Marketing Research* 45 (6): 633–44. doi:10.1509 /jmkr.45.6.633.

Mazza, M. C., Dynan, L., Siegel, R. M., and Tucker, A. L. (2018). Nudging Healthier Choices in a Hospital Cafeteria: Results from a Field Study. *Health Promotion Practice*. 19 (6): 925–34. doi:10.1177/1524839917740119.

McAlister, A. R. and Kononova, A. (2020). Consumption of Fruits, Vegetables, and Nuts Can Be Increased When Multitasking with Screen Devices. *Health Communication*. 37 (2): 141–51. doi:10.1080/10410236.2020.1827527.

Mecheva, M. V., Rieger, M., Sparrow, R., Prafiantini, E., and Agustina, R. (2021). Snacks, Nudges and Asymmetric Peer Influence: Evidence from Food Choice Experiments with Children in Indonesia. *Journal of Health Economics* 79: 102508. doi:10.1016/j.jhealeco .2021.102508.

Medveď, J., Nemec, J., and Vítek, L. (2005). Public Health Insurance and Its Failures in the Czech Republic and Slovakia: The Role of State. *Prague Economic Pares* 14 (1): 64–81. doi:10.18267/j.pep.253.

Meričková-Mikušová, B. and Jakuš Muthová, N. (2019). Bounded Rationality of Individual Action in the Consumption of Public Goods. *Nispacee Journal of Public Administration and Policy* 12 (2): 157–94. doi:10.2478/nispa-2019-0018.

Meričková-Mikušová, B. and Jakuš Muthová, N. (2018). Consumer Preferences and Willingness to Pay for Public Goods. In *Proceedings of the 22nd International Conference Current Trends in Public Sector Research 2018*, edited by P. Dvoráková, B. Baisa, 83–90. Brno: Masarykova Univerzita.

Mertl, J. (2014). The Impact of Longevity on Health Care Systems. *European Research Studies Journal* 17 (1): 85–100. doi:10.35808/ersj/412.

Mertl, J. (2013). Trends of Health Care Financing in OECD Countries. In *Teoretické a Praktické aspekty veřejných finance*, 7. Prague: Vysoká škola ekonomická.

Mertl, J. (2015). The Transformation of Czech Public Health Insurance to Earmarked Health Tax. *In Current Trends in the Public Sector Research,* 258–65. Brno: Masarykova Univerzita.

Mertl, J. (2016). *K. Lacina: Public Management.* Review of monograph. Prague: VŠFS Eupress.

Mikkelsen, Bent E., Sudzina, F., Ørnbo, Line E., Tvedebrink and Tena Doktor, O. (2021). Does Visibility Matter? – A Simple Nudge Reduces the Purchase of Sugar Sweetened Beverages in Canteen Drink Coolers. *Food Quality and Preference* 92: 104190. doi:10.1016/j.foodqual.2021.104190.

Mises, L. (2018). *Lidské jednání: Pojednání o ekonomii [Human Behaviour: An Essay on Economics]*. An anthology edited and translated by Šíma, J. et kol. Prague: Liberální institut.

Mistura, M., Fetterly, N., Rhodes, R. E., Tomlin, D. and Taylor, P.-J. (2019). Examining the Efficacy of a 'Feasible' Nudge Intervention to Increase the Purchase of Vegetables by First Year University Students (17–19 Years of Age) in British Columbia: A Pilot Study. *Nutrients* 11 (8): 1786. doi:10.3390/nu11081786.

Mohr, B., Dolgopolova, I., and Roosen, J. (2019). The Influence of Sex and Self-Control on The Efficacy of Nudges in Lowering the Energy Content of Food During a Fast Food Order. *Appetite* 141:104314. doi:10.1016/j.appet.2019.06.006.

Montagni, I., Prevot, F., Castro, Z., Goubel, B., Perrin, L., Oppert, J.-M. and Fontvieille, A.-M. (2020). Using Positive Nudge to Promote Healthy Eating at Worksite. *Journal of Occupational and Environmental Medicine* 62 (6): 260–6. doi:10.1097/JOM .0000000000001861.

Morewedge, C. K., and Giblin, C. E. (2015). Explanations of the Endowment Effect: An Integrative Review. *Trends in Cognitive Sciences* 19 (6): 339–48. doi:10.1016/j. tics.2015.04.004.

Morewedge, C. K., Gilbert, D. T., and Wilson, T. D. (2005). The Least Likely of Times: How Remembering the Past Biases Forecasts of the Future. *Psychological Science* 16 (8): 626–30. http://www.jstor.org/stable/40064281.

Morren, M., Mol, Jantsje, M., Blasch, J. E. and Malek, Ž. (2021). Changing Diets – Testing the Impact of Knowledge and Information Nudges on Sustainable Dietary Choices. *Journal of Environmental Psychology* 75:101610. doi:10.1016/j.jenvp.2021.101610.

Mors, M. R., Polet, I. A., Vingerhoeds M. H., Perez-Cueto, F. J. A., and de Wijk, R. A. (2018). Can Food Choice Be Influenced by Priming with Food Odours? *Food Quality and Preference* 66: 148–52. doi:10.1016/j.appet.2021.105772.

Muñoz-Vilches, Naomí C., Van Trijp, Hans C. M. and Piqueras-Fiszman, B. (2019). The Impact of Instructed Mental Simulation on Wanting and Choice Between Vice and Virtue Food Products. *Food Quality and Preference* 73:182–91. doi:10.1016/j.foodqual.2018.11.010.

Nagatomo, W., Saito, J. and Kondo, N. (2019). Effectiveness of a Low-Value Financial-Incentive Program for Increasing Vegetable-Rich Restaurant Meal Selection and Reducing Socioeconomic Inequality: A Cluster Crossover Trial. *Int J Behav Nutr Phys Act* 16: 81. doi:10.1186/s12966-019-0830-5.

Nagatsu, M. (2015). History of Behavioral Economics. In *International Encyclopedia of the Social & Behavioral Sciences*, 443–9. doi:10.1016/B978-0-08-097086-8.03053-1.

Németh, B., Józwiak-Hagymásy, J., Kovács, G., Kovács, A., Demjén, T. et al. (2018). Cost-Effectiveness of Possible Future Smoking Cessation Strategies in Hungary: Results from the Equiptmod. *Addiction* 113: 76–86. doi:10.1111/add.14089.

Neumann, J. von and Morgenstern, O. (2004). *Theory of Games and Economic Behavior.* Princeton: Princeton University.

Novotný, R. (2018). Je lepší tisícovku neztratit, než tisícovku najít? [Is it better not to lose a thousand than to find a thousand?], Investujeme.cz, https://www.investujeme.cz/clanky/lepsi-tisicovku-neztratit-nez-tisicovku-najit.

Odean, T. (1998). Volume, Volatility, Price, and Profit When All Traders Are Above Average. *Journal of Finance* 53 (6): 1887–1934. doi:10.1111/0022-1082.00078.

OECD. (2019). *The Heavy Burden of Obesity: The Economics of Prevention* (Oct 10). doi.org/10.1787/67450d67-en.

OECD. (2018). *Economic Surveys Czech Republic* (July 2018). http://www.oecd.org.

Ogaki, M. and S. Tanaka (2017). *Behavioral Economics: Toward a New Economics by Integration with Traditional Economics.* New York: Springer.

Ohlhausen, P. and N. Langen (2020). When a Combination of Nudges Decreases Sustainable Food Choices Out-Of-Home – The Example of Food Decoys and Descriptive Name Labels. *Foods* 9 (5): 557. doi:10.3390/foods9050557.

Ochrana, F. (1998). Nový duch vědy Gastona Bachelarda [Gaston Bachelard's New Spirit of Science]. *Filosofický časopis* 46 (2): 203–13.

Ojwang, Sylvester O., Otieno, David J., Okello, Julius J., Nyikal, Rose A. and Muoki, P. (2021). The Role of Targeted Nutrition Education of Preschoolers and Caregivers on Sustained Consumption of Biofortified Orange-Fleshed Sweetpotato in Kenya. *Current Developments in Nutrition* 5 (8). doi:10.1093/cdn/nzab096.

Oliver, A. (2011). Is Nudge an Effective Public Health Strategy to Tackle Obesity? Yes. *BMJ* (Apr 13): 342. doi:10.1136/bmj.d2168.

Oliver, A. (2013). From Nudging to Budging: Using Behavioural Economics to Inform Public Sector Policy. *Journal of Social Policy* 42 (4): 685–700. doi:10.1017/S0047279413000299.

Otto, A. S., Davis, B., Wakefield, K., Clarkson, J. J. and Inman, Jeffrey J. (2020), Consumer Strategies to Improve the Efficacy of Posted Calorie Information: How Provincial Norms Nudge Consumers to Healthier Consumption. *J Consum Aff* 54: 311-41. doi:10.1111/joca.12272.

Ozturk, O. D., Frongillo, E. A., Blake Ch. E., Mcinnes, M. M. and Turner-McGrievy, G. (2020). Before the Lunch Line: Effectiveness of Behavioral Economic Interventions for Pre-Commitment on Elementary School Children's Food Choices. *Journal of Economic Behavior and Organization* 176: 597–618. doi:10.1016/j.jebo.2020.03.027.

Pallier, G., Wilkinson, R., Danthiir, V., Kleitman, S., Knezevic, G., Stankov, L., and Roberts, R. D. (2002). The Role of Individual Differences in the Accuracy of Confidence Judgments. *Journal of General Psychology* 129 (3): 257–99. doi:10.1080/00221300209602099.

Peng-Li, D., Byrne, D. V., Chan, R. C. K., and Qian J. W. (2020) The Influence of Taste-Congruent Soundtracks on Visual Attention and Food Choice: A Cross-Cultural Eye-Tracking Study in Chinese and Danish Consumers. *Food Quality and Preference* 85:103962. doi.org/10.1016/j.foodqual.2020.103962.

Pérez-Escamilla, R. (2020). Breastfeeding in the 21st Century: How We Can Make It Work. *Social Science & Medicine* 244: 112331. doi:10.1016/j.socscimed.2019.05.036.

Perušicová, J., et al. (2011). *Diabetes mellitus 2. typu* [Type 2 Diabetes mellitus]. Prague: Geum.

Petit, O., Velasco, C. and Spence, C. (2018). Are Large Portions Always Bad? Using The Delboeuf Illusion on Food Packaging to Nudge Consumer Behavior. *Mark Lett* 29: 435–49. doi: 10.1007/s11002-018-9473-6.

Petticrew, M., Maani, N., Pettigrew, L., Rutter, H., and Van Schalkwyk, M. C. (2020), Dark Nudges and Sludge in Big Alcohol: Behavioral Economics, Cognitive Biases, and Alcohol Industry Corporate Social Responsibility. *The Milbank Quarterly* 98: 1290–1328. doi: 10.1111/1468-0009.12475.

Plous, S. (1993) *The Psychology of Judgment and Decision Making*. New York: McGraw-Hill.

Polacsek, M., Moran, A., Thorndike, A. N., Boulos, R. et al. (2018). A Supermarket Double-Dollar Incentive Program Increases Purchases of Fresh Fruits and Vegetables Among Low-Income Families with Children: The Healthy Double Study. *Journal of Nutrition Education and Behavior* 50 (3): 217–28. doi:10.1016/j.jneb.2017.09.013.

Policastro, P., Palm, T., Schwartz, J., and Chapman, G. (2017). Targeted Calorie Message Promotes Healthy Beverage Consumption Better Than Charity Incentive. *Obesity* 25 (8): 1428–34. doi:10.1002/oby.21885.

Prainsack, B. (2020). The Value of Healthcare Data: to Nudge, or Not? *Policy Studies* 41 (5): 547–62. doi:10.1002/oby.21885.

Prelec, D. and Loewenstein, G. (1998). The Red and the Black: Mental Accounting of Savings and Debt. *Marketing Science* 17 (1): 4–28, doi.org/10.1287/mksc.17.1.4.

Prelec, D. and Simester, D. (2001). Always Leave Home Without It: A Further Investigation of The Credit-Card Effect on Willingness to Pay. *Marketing Letters* 12: 5–12. doi:10.1023/A:1008196717017.

Preston, M. G. and Baratta, M. (1948). An Experimental Study of The Auction-Value of An Uncertain Outcome. *American Journal of Psychology* 61 (2): 183–93. doi:10.2307/1416964.

Proulx, D. and. Savage, D. A. (2020). What Determines End-of-Life Attitudes? Revisiting The Dutch Experience. *Soc Indic Res* 152: 1085–125. doi:10.1007/s11205-020-02475-9.

Prusaczyk, E., Earle, M., and Hodson, G. (2021). A Brief Nudge or Education Intervention Delivered Online Can Increase Willingness to Order a Beef-Mushroom Burger. *Food Quality and Preference* 87: 104045. doi:10.1016/j.foodqual.2020.104045.

Raghoebar, S., Van Rongen, S., Lie, R. and De Vet, E. (2019). Identifying Social Norms in Physical Aspects of Food Environments: A Photo Study. *Appetite* 143: 104414. doi:10.1016/j.appet.2019.104414.

Read, D., and Loewenstein, G. (1995). Diversification Bias: Explaining the Discrepancy in Variety Seeking Between Combined and Separated Choices. *Journal of Experimental Psychology: Applied* 1 (1): 34–49. doi:10.1037/1076-898X.1.1.34.

Reach, G. (2016). Patient Education, Nudge, and Manipulation: Defining the Ethical Conditions of the Person-Centered Model of Care. *Patient Preference and Adherence* 10:459–68. doi:10.2147/ppa.s99627.

Reijnen, E., Kühne, S. J., Von Gugelberg, H. M. et al. (2019). Nudged to a Menu Position: The Role of I'm Loving It! *J Consum Policy* 42: 441–53. doi:10.1007/s10603 -019-09413-4

Reinoso-Carvalho, F., Campo, R., De Luca, M., and Velasco, C. (2021). Toward Healthier Cookie Habits: Assessing the Role of Packaging Visual Appearance in the Expectations for Dietary Cookies in Digital Environments. *Frontiers in Psychology* 12: 679443. doi:10.3389/fpsyg.2021.679443.

Reisch L., Sunstein, C., and W. Gwozdz (2016) Beyond Carrots and Sticks: Europeans Support Health Nudges. *Food Policy* 69 (May): 1–10. doi.org/10.1016/j.foodpol .2017.01.007.

Reynolds, J. P., Archer, S., Pilling, M., Kenny, M., Hollands, G. J., and Marteau, T. M. (2019). Public Acceptability of Nudging and Taxing to Reduce Consumption of Alcohol, Tobacco, and Food: A Population-Based Survey Experiment. *Social Science and Medicine* 236: 112395. doi:10.1016/j.socscimed.2019.112395.

Rick, S. (2018). Tightwads and Spendthrifts: An Interdisciplinary Review. *Financial Planning Review* 1 (September 19). doi: 10.1002/cfp2.1010.

Rising, J. C. and Bol, N. (2017). Nudging Our Way to a Healthier Population: The Effect of Calorie Labeling and Self-Control on Menu Choices of Emerging Adult. *Health Communication* 32 (8): 1032–8. doi:10.1080/10410236.2016.1217452.

Roberto, C. A. (2020). How Psychological Insights Can Inform Food Policies to Address Unhealthy Eating Habits. *American Psychologist* 75 (2): 265–73. doi:10.1037 /amp0000554.

Robinson, E. and Kersbergen, I. (2018). Portion Size and Later Food Intake: Evidence on the "Normalizing" Effect of Reducing Food Portion Sizes, *The American Journal of Clinical Nutrition* 107 (4): 640–6. doi:10.1093/ajcn/nqy013.

Rogus, S. (2018). Examining The Influence of Perceived and Objective Time Constraints on the Quality of Household Food Purchases. *Appetite* 130: 268–73. doi:10.1016 /j.appet.2018.08.025.

Rookhuijzen, M. van and De Vet, E. (2020). Nudging Healthy Eating in Dutch Sports Canteens: A Multi-Method Case Study. *Public Health Nutrition* 24 (2): 327-37. doi:0.1017/S1368980020002013.

Rowley, J. and Spence, C. (2018). Does the Visual Composition of a Dish Influence the Perception of Portion Size and Hedonic Preference? *Appetite* 128 (*Sep 1): 79–86. doi: 10.1016/j.appet.2018.06.005.

Ruwende, J. (2019). *GP-Endorsed Text Reminders Help Increase Cervical Screening Attendance in London*, https://phescreening.blog.gov.uk/2019/07/15/gp-endorsed-text-reminders-help-increase-cervical-screening-attendance-in-london/.

Rybka, J. (2007). *Diabetes Mellitus– komplikace a přidružená onemocnění: diagnostické a léčebné postupy* [Diabetes mellitus – Complications and Associated Diseases: Diagnostic and Therapeutic Procedures]. Prague: Grada.

Sabatier, P. A. (ed.) (1999). *Theories of The Policy Process*. Boulder: Westview Press.

Samek, A. (2019). Gifts and Goals: Behavioral Nudges to Improve Child Food Choice at School. *Journal of Economic Behavior and Organization* 164: 1-12. doi:10.1016/j.jebo .2019.05.008.

Santos, O., Alarcão, V., Santos, and Feteira-Santos, R. (2020). Impact of Different Front-of-Pack Nutrition Labels on Online Food Choices. *Appetite* 154: 104795. doi:10.1016/j.appet.2020.104795.

Saulais, L., Massey, C., Perez-Cueto, F. J. A., Appleton, K. M. et al. (2019). When Are "Dish of The Day" Nudges Most Effective to Increase Vegetable Selection? *Food Policy* 85: 15–27. doi:10.1016/j.foodpol.2019.04.003.

Savani, M. M. (2019). Can Commitment Contracts Boost Participation in Public Health Programmes? *Journal of Behavioral and Experimental Economics* 82: 101457. doi:10.1016/j.socec.2019.101457.

Seward, M. W. and Soled, Derek R. (2020). Unintended Consequences in Traffic-Light Food Labeling: A Call for Mixed Methods in Public Health Research. *Journal of American College Health*. 68 (5): 465-67. doi:10.1080/07448481.2019.1583238.

Shampanier, K., Mazar, N., and Ariely D. (2007). Zero As a Special Price: The True Value of Free Products. *Marketing Science* 26: 742-57. doi:10.1287/mksc.1060.0254.

Shang, J. and R. Croson (2009). Field Experiments in Charitable Contribution: The Impact of Social Influence on The Voluntary Provision of Public Goods. *The Economic Journal* 119: 1422-39. doi: 10.1111/j.1468-0297.2009.02267.x.

Sharot, T. (2011). The Optimism Bias. *Current Biology* 21 (23): 941-5. doi:10.1016/j.cub.2011.10.030.

Sharps M. A., Hetherington M. M., Blundell-Birtill P., Rolls B. J. and Evans C. E. (2019). The Effectiveness of a Social Media Intervention for Reducing Portion Sizes in Young Adults and Adolescents. *Digital Health*. doi:10.1177/2055207619878076.

Shiller, R. (2014). Speculative Asset Prices. *The American Economic Review* 104 (6): 1486-1517. doi:104. 10.1257/aer.104.6.1486.

Shiv, B., Carmon, Z., and Ariely, D. (2005). Placebo Effects of Marketing Actions: Consumers May Get What They Pay For. *Journal of Marketing Research* 42 (4): 383-393.

Schneider, A. and Ingram, H. (1990) Behavioral Assumptions of Policy Tools. *The Journal of Politics* 52 (2): 510–29. doi:10.2139/ssrn.707541.

Schwartz, B. (2004). *The Paradox of Choice: Why More Is Less*. New York: Harper Collins.

Sihvonen, J. and Luomala, H. (2017). Hear What I Appreciate: Activation of Consumption Motives for Healthier Food Choices Across Different Value Segments. *The International Review of Retail, Distribution and Consumer Research* 27 (5): 502–514. doi:10.1080/09593969.2017.1383290.

Simon, H. A. (1947/1997). *Administrative Behavior: A Study of Decision-making Process in Administrative Organisations*. New York: Simon and Schuster.

Slapø, H. B. and Karevold, K. I. (2019). Simple Eco-Labels to Nudge Customers Toward the Most Environmentally Friendly Warm Dishes: An Empirical Study in a Cafeteria Setting. *Frontiers in Sustainable Food Systems* 3 (40). doi:10.3389/Fsufs.2019.00040.

Slovic, P. (1995): Construction of Preference. American Psychologist 50 (5): 364-71. doi:10.1037/0003-066X.50.5.364.

Smith, M. J. and Toprakkiran, N. (2018). Behavioural Insights, Nudge and the Choice Environment in Obesity Policy. *Policy Studies* 40 (2): 173-87. doi:10.1080/01442872.2018.1554806.

Sogari G., Li J., Lefebvre M., Menozzi D., Pellegrini N., Cirelli M., Gómez M. I., Mora C. (2019). The Influence of Health Messages in Nudging Consumption of Whole Grain Pasta. *Nutrients* 11 (12): 2993. doi:10.3390/Nu11122993.

Soofi, M., Najafi F. and Karami-Matin B. (2020). Using Insights from Behavioral Economics to Mitigate the Spread of Covid-19. *Appl Health Econ Health Policy* 18 (3): 345-50. doi:10.1007/S40258-020-00595-4.

Soofi, M., Akbari Sari, A., Najafi, F. (2020). The Effect of Individual Time Preferences on Smoking Behavior: Insights from Behavioral Economics. *Iranian Journal of Public Health. Volume* 49 (9): 1787-95. doi:10.18502/ijph.v49i9.4100.

Soofi, M., Sari, A. A., Rezaei, S., Hajizadeh, M. and Najafi, F. (2019), Individual Time Preferences and Obesity: A Behavioral Economics Analysis Using a Quasi-Hyperbolic Discounting Approach. *International Journal of Social Economics* 47 (1): 16–26. doi:10.1108/IJSE-04-2019-0271.

Sperl-Hillen J., Asche S., Ruanpeng D., Ekstrom H., and O'Connor, P. (2017). Primary Care Provider Use Rates of a Clinical Decision Support Tool and Change in Diabetes Performance Measures. *J Patient Cent Res Rev.* 4 (3): 155. doi:10.17294/2330-0698.1484.

Stamos, A., Goddyn, H., Andronikidis A., and Dewitte S. (2018). Pre-Exposure to Tempting Food Reduces Subsequent Snack Consumption in Healthy-Weight but Not in Obese-Weight Individuals. *Frontiers in Psychology* 9: 685. doi:10.3389/fpsyg.2018 .00685.

Stämpfli Aline E., Stöckli S., Brunner, and Thomas A. (2017). A Nudge in a Healthier Direction: How Environmental Cues Help Restrained Eaters Pursue Their Weight-Control Goal. *Appetite* 110: 94-102. doi:10.1016/j.appet.2016.11.037.

Starke, A. D., Willemsen, M. C. and Trattner, C. (2021). Nudging Healthy Choices in Food Search Through Visual Attractiveness. *Frontiers in Artificial Intelligence* 4: 621743. doi:10.1016/j.appet.2016.11.037.

Statistics on Obesity, Physical Activity and Diet, England (2020). https://digital.nhs.uk.

State of Health in the EU. Česko. Zdravotní profil země [Czechia. Country Health Profile]. (2019). https://eurohealthobservatory.who.int/publications/m/czechia-country-health -profile-2019.

Statistika vybraných ekonomických témat [Statistics of selected economic topics]. (2020). Ústav zdravotnických informací a statistiky ČR. https://www.uzis.cz/index. php?pg=vystupy--statistika-vybranych-ekonomickych-temat-- ekonomicke-vysledky.

Strugnell, C. (1997). Colour and Its Role in Sweetness Perception. *Appetite* 28 (1): 85. doi:10.1006/appe.1996.0065.

Stuber, J. M., Mackenbach, J. D., de Boer, F. E. et al. (2020). Reducing Cardiometabolic Risk in Adults with a Low Socioeconomic Position: Protocol of the Supreme Nudge Parallel Cluster-Randomised Controlled Supermarket Trial. *Nutr J* 19 (1): 46. doi:10.1186/s12937-020-00562-8.

Stuber, Josine M., Hoenink, Jody C., Beulens, W. J., Mackenbach, Joreintje D., and Lakerveld, J. (2021). Shifting Toward a Healthier Dietary Pattern Through Nudging and Pricing Strategies: A Secondary Analysis of a Randomized Virtual Supermarket Experiment. *The American Journal of Clinical Nutrition* 114 (2): 628–37. doi:10.1093/ajcn /nqab057.

Sullivan, P. S., Lansky, A., Drake, A. (2004). Failure to Return for Hiv Test Results Among Persons at High Risk for Hiv Infection: Results from a Multistate Interview Project. *Jaids Journal of Acquired Immune Deficiency Syndromes* 35 (5): 511–8. doi:10.1097/00126334-200404150-00009.

Sumner, W. G. (1906). *Folkways a Study of The Sociological Importance of Usages Manners Customs Mores and Morals.* New York: Ginn and Company.

Sunstein, C. R. (1996). Social Norms and Social Roles. *Columbia Law Review* 96 (4): 903–68. doi:10.2307/1123430.

Svačina, Š. (2010). *Diabetologie [Diabetology].* Prague: Triton.

Swanton, T., Gainsbury, S., and Blaszczynski, A. (2019). The Role of Financial Institutions in Gambling. *International Gambling Studies* 19 (2): 1–22. doi:10.1080 /14459795.2019.1575450.

Szakály, Z., Soós, M., Balsa-Budai, N., Kovács, S., and Kontor, E. (2020). The Effect of An Evaluative Label on Consumer Perception of Cheeses in Hungary, *Foods* 9 (5): 563. doi:10.3390/foods9050563.

Tangari, Heintz A., Banerjee, S., and Verma, S. (2019). Making a Good Thing Even Better? The Impact of Claim Congruency on Competing Product Goals and Consumer Evaluations. *Journal of Business Research* 101: 12-22. doi:10.1016/j.jbusres.2019.03.059.

Tani Y., Fujiwara T., Ochi M., Isumi, A., and Kato, T. (2018) Does Eating Vegetables at Start of Meal Prevent Childhood Overweight in Japan? A Child Study. *Front. Pediatr* 6: 134. doi:10.3389/fped.2018.00134.

Thaler, R. H. (1999). Mental Accounting Matters. Journal of Behavioral Decision Making. *J. Behav. Decis. Making* 12: 183–206. doi:10.1002/(SICI)1099-0771(199909)12:3<183::AID-BDM318>3.0.CO;2-F.

Thaler, R. and Sunstein, C. (2009). *Nudge: Improving Decisions About Health, Wealth, and Happiness.* New Haven: Yale University Press.

Thaler, R. H. (2005). *Advances in Behavioral Finance* (Volume II. Student Edition). Princeton: Princeton University Press.

Thaler, R. H. (2015). *Misbehaving: The Making of Behavioral Economics.* New York: W. W. Norton & Company.

Thaler, R. H. (2015). *The Power of Nudges, for Good and Bad.* The New York Times.

Thaler, R. H. (2016). Behavioral Economics: Past, Present and Future. Advances in Behavioral Economics, *American Economic Review* 106 (7): 1577–1600. doi:10.1257 /aer.106.7.1577.

Thaler, R. H. and Benartzi, S. (2004). Save More Tomorrow: Using Behavioral Economics to Increase Employee Saving. *Journal of Political Economy* 112:164–87. doi:10.1086/380085.

Thaler, R. H. and Sunstein, C. (2008). *Nudge: Improving Decisions About Health, Wealth, and Happiness.* New Haven: Yale University Press.

Theodoulou, S. Z. and Cahn, M. A. (1995). *Public Policy. Essential Readings.* Hoboken: Prentice Hall.

Thorndike, A. N. (2020). Healthy Choice Architecture in The Supermarket: Does It Work? *Social Science and Medicine* 266:113459. doi:10.1016/j.socscimed.2020.113459.

Thorndike, A. N., Sonnenberg, L., Riis, J., Barraclough, S. and Levy, D. E. (2012). A 2phase Labeling and Choice Architecture Intervention to Improve Healthy Food and Beverage Choices. *American Journal of Public Health* 102 (3): 527–33. doi:10.2105/AJPH .2011.300391.

Thunström, L., Gilbert, B., Ritten, and Chian, J. (2018). Nudges That Hurt Those Already Hurting – Distributional and Unintended Effects of Salience Nudges. *Journal of Economic Behavior and Organization* 153: 267-82. doi:10.1016/j.jebo.2018.07.005.

Tijssen, I., Zandstra, E. H., Graaf, C. de, and Jager, G. (2017). Why a Light product Package Should Not Be Light Blue: Effects of Package Colour on Perceived Healthiness and Attractiveness of Sugar – and Fat-Reduced Products. *Food Quality and Preference* 59: 46-58. doi:10.1016/j.foodqual.2017.01.019.

Tonkin, M., Kemps, E., Prichard, I., Polivy, J., Herman, P. C., and Tiggemann, M. (2019). It's All in the Timing: The Effect of a Healthy Food Cue on Food Choices from a Pictorial Menu. *Appetite* 139: 105-9. doi:10.1016/j.appet.2019.04.026.

Torma, G., Aschemann-Witzel, J., and Thøgersen, J. (2018). I Nudge Myself: Exploring 'Self-Nudging' Strategies to Drive Sustainable Consumption Behaviour. *Int J Consum Stud.* 42: 141–54. doi:10.1111/ijcs.12404.

Trakman, G., Staley, K., Forsyth, A., Devlin, B., Skiadopoulos, A., Pearce, K., Nicholson M., and Belski, R. (2021) Healthy-Canteen Displays: A Tactic to Encourage

Community Sport Canteens to Provide Healthier Food and Beverage Options. *Int. J. Environ. Res. Public Health* 18 (19): 10194. doi:10.3390/ijerph181910194.

Tranfield, D., Denyer, D., and Smart, P. (2003), Towards a Methodology for Developing Evidence-Informed Management Knowledge by Means of Systematic Review. *British Journal of Management* 14 (3): 207–22. doi:10.1111/1467-8551.00375.

Tversky, A. and D. Kahneman (1971). Belief in the Law of Small Numbers. *Psychological Bulletin* 76 (2): 105–10. doi:10.1037/h0031322.

Tversky, A., Kahneman, D. (1974). Judgment Under Uncertainty: Heuristics and Biases. *Science (New Series)* 185 (4157): 1124–31. doi:10.1126/science.185.4157.1124.

Tversky, A., Kahneman, D. (1981). The Framing of Decisions and the Psychology of Choice. *Science* 211 (4481): 453–8. doi:10.1126/Science.7455683.

Vandenbroele, J., Slabbinck, H., Kerckhove, Van A., and Vermeir, I. (2018). Curbing Portion Size Effects by Adding Smaller Portions at the Point of Purchase. *Food Quality and Preference* 64: 82–7. doi:10.1016/j.foodqual.2017.10.015.

Vandenbroele, J., Slabbinck, H., Kerckhove, Van A., and Vermeir, I. (2021). Mock Meat in the Butchery: Nudging Consumers Toward Meat Substitutes. *Organizational Behavior and Human Decision Processes* 163: 105–116. doi:10.1016/j.obhdp.2019.09.004.

Velema, E., Vyth, E. L., Hoekstra, T., Steenhuis, and Ingrid H.-M. (2018). Nudging and Social Marketing Techniques Encourage Employees to Make Healthier Food Choices: A Randomized Controlled Trial in 30 Worksite Cafeterias in The Netherlands. *The American Journal of Clinical Nutrition* 107 (2): 236–46. doi:10.1093/ajcn/nqx045.

Venema, T. A. G., Kroese, F. M., Verplanken, B., De Ridder, and Denise T. D. (2020). The (Bitter) Sweet Taste of Nudge Effectiveness: The Role of Habits in a Portion Size Nudge, a Proof-of-Concept Study. *Appetite* 151: 104699. doi:10.1016/j.appet.2020 .104699.

Vermote, M., Nys, J., Versele, V., D'Hondt, E., Deforche, B., Clarys, P., and Deliens, T. (2020). The Effect of Nudges Aligned with the Renewed Flemish Food Triangle on the Purchase of Fresh Fruits: An On-Campus Restaurant Experiment. *Appetite* 144: 104479. doi:10.1016/j.appet.2019.104479.

Vermote, M., Versele, V., Stok, M. et al. (2018). The Effect of a Portion Size Intervention on French Fries Consumption, Plate Waste, Satiety and Compensatory Caloric Intake: An On-Campus Restaurant Experiment. *Nutr J* 17: 43. doi:10.1186/s12937-018-0352-z.

Villinger, K., Wahl, D., Engel, K. et al. (2021). Nudging Sugar Portions: A Real-World Experiment. *BMC Nutrition* 7: 65. doi:10.1186/s40795-021-00473-9.

Vítek, L. (2012). Regulatory Impact Assessment in the Czech Republic. *European Financial and Accounting Journal* 7 (3): 63–78. doi:10.18267/j.efaj.5.

Vrabková, I. and Vaňková, I. (2015). *Evaluation Models of Efficiency and Quality of Bed Care in Hospitals*. Ostrava: VŠB-TU.

Walker, L. A., Chambers, C. D., Veling, H., and Lawrence, N. S. (2019). *Cognitive and Environmental Interventions to Encourage Healthy Eating: Evidence-Based Recommendations for Public Health Policy*. Royal Social Open Science. doi:10.1098/rsos.190624.

Wan, X., Qiu, L., and Wang, C. (2021). A Virtual Reality-Based Study of Color Contrast to Encourage More Sustainable Food Choices. *Applied Psychology: Health and Well-Being* 14 (2): 591–605. doi.org/10.1111/aphw.12321.

Weber, M. and Havelka, M. (2009). *Metodologie, sociologie a politika*. Prague: OIKOYMENH.

Wilkinson, N. and Klaes, M. (2012). *An Introduction to Behavioral Economics*. New York: Palgrave Macmillan.

Wilson, T. D., Gilbert, D. T. (2003). Affective Forecasting. *Advances in Experimental Social Psychology* 35: 345–411. doi:10.1016/S0065-2601(03)01006-2.

Winkler, G., Berger, B., Filipiak-Pittroff, B., Hartmann, A., and Streber, A. (2018). Small Changes in Choice Architecture in Self-Service Cafeterias. Do They Nudge Consumers Towards Healthier Food Choices? *Ernahrungs Umschau* 65 (10): 546–54. doi:10.4455 /eu.2018.038.

Witman, A., Acquah, J., Alva, M., Hoerger, T., and Romaire, M. (2018). Medicaid Incentives for Preventing Chronic Disease: Effects of Financial Incentives for Smoking Cessation. *Health Services Research* 53 (6): 5016–34. doi:10.1111/1475-6773.12994.

Wyse, R., Gabrielyan, G., Wolfenden, L., Yoong, S., Swigert, J. et al. (2019). Can Changing the Position of Online Menu Items Increase Selection of Fruit and Vegetable Snacks? A Cluster Randomized Trial Within an Online Canteen Ordering System in Australian Primary Schools. *The American Journal of Clinical Nutrition* 109 (5): 1422–30. doi:10.1093/ajcn/nqy351.

Wyse, R., Delaney, T., Stacey, F. et al. (2021). Effectiveness of a Multistrategy Behavioral Intervention to Increase the Nutritional Quality of Primary School Students' Web-Based Canteen Lunch Orders (Click & Crunch): Cluster Randomized Controlled Trial. *J Med Internet Res* 23 (9). doi:10.2196/26054.

Zeballos, E., Mancino, L., and Lin, B.-H. (2020). Does How You Pay Influence the Share of Healthy Items That You Buy? Assessing Differences in Nutritional Quality of Food Purchases by Payment Type. *Food Policy* 92: 101886. doi:10.1016/j.foodpol.2020.101886.

Zhou, X., Perez-Cueto, Federico J. A., Dos Santos, Q., Bredie, Wender L. P. et al. (2019). Promotion of Novel Plant-Based Dishes Among Older Consumers Using the "Dish of the Day" As a Nudging Strategy in 4 EU Countries. *Food Quality and Preference* 75: 260–72. doi:10.1016/j.foodqual.2018.12.003.